FROM SELLING TO CO-CREATING

BIS Publishers
Building Het Sieraad
Postjesweg 1
1057 DT Amsterdam
The Netherlands
T +31 (0)20 515 02 30
F +31 (0)20 515 02 39
bis@bispublishers.nl
www.bispublishers.nl

design: Marco Simoni

ISBN 978 90 6369 351 0

RÉGIS LEMMENS   BILL DONALDSON   JAVIER MARCOS

FROM SELLING TO CO-CREATING

BISPUBLISHERS

4

The task of writing a book is seldom the result of the work or the thinking of one individual. The research that underpins the book and ideas presented in this volume are the consequence of genuine friendship and support received from colleagues and clients, and of inspiring insights that emerged in our discussions and engagement with them. We are grateful to the academics and professionals we have been privileged to work with. We are also indebted to Cranfield School of Management, TiasNimbas Business School and the Sales Management Association in the Netherlands. They made our early research project possible and provided in the early beginning the needed support to get us going. We are **especially thankful** to:

Prof. Dr. Lynette Ryals (Cranfield School of Management)
Prof. Neil Rackham (Cranfield School of Management)
Dr. Sue Holt (Cranfield School of Management)
Mark Davies (Cranfield School of Management)
Prof. Dr. Will Reijnders (TiasNimbas Business School)
Prof. Dr. Carla Koen (TiasNimbas Business School)
Prof. Dr. Rudy Moenaert (TiasNimbas Business School)
Geert-Jan Peters (TiasNimbas Business School)
Menno Jansen (TiasNimbas Business School)
Stefan Smits (TiasNimbas Business School)
Eiso Bleeker (Sales Management Association)
Dick van Nes (Sales Management Association)
Thijs Verhees (Sales Management Association / SalesMediagroep)
Berry Veldhoen (Sales Management Association)
Patricia Coucheir (Antwerp Management School)
Dorinela Munteanu (Antwerp Management School)
Prof. Dr. Patrick Kenis (Antwerp Management School)
Prof. Jamie Anderson (Antwerp Management School)
Wendy Freriks (Ricoh)
Bruno Winnen (Sony Europe)
Peter De Clerck (LMS / Siemens)
Joop Groen (TNO Life Sciences)
Hendrik Thooft (Bekaert)
Lieven Somers (Bekaert)
Michel Vandevelde (Bekaert)
Filip Verhoeve (Bekaert)
Koen Cremmery (Bekaert)

Frank van Nistelrooij (Watermelt)
Sander Van den Born (CGI)
Marieke Fizaan (Vion Food)
Geert Van De Wiele (Pepper+Fuchs)
Marc Van Pelt (Pepper+Fuchs)
Serge Proost (Suzuki Belgium)
Phil Squire (Consalia)
Ian Helps (Consalia)
Udo P. Malter (MLP Finanzdienstleistungen AG)
Colin England (Rolls-Royce)
Andy Lane (Rolls-Royce)
Pablo Perversi and the UFS team (Unilever)
Vatsan Govindarajan (SAP)
Richard Vincent (HP)
John Baker (Geodis Wilson)
Vince McShane (Geodis Wilson)
Ralph Baillie (Merck)
Alan Finkelstein (Merck)
Bruno M. Wattenbergh (Impulse Brussels)
Juan Bossicard (Impulse Brussels)
Stephanie Robin (Impulse Brussels)
Jonathan Bayens (Impulse Brussels)
Sandra Gole (Voka / MBA highlights)
Piet Salens (EMG Edit)
Gude Verhaert (Kluwer Training)
Patrick Bamps (Patenka)
Luc Francis Jacobs (Nixxis)
Tom Vanderbiesen (Sales Cubes)
Johan Vranckx (Sales Cubes)
Synnove Johansson (Sales Cubes)
Peter Manet (Yontec / MBA highlights)
Chris Timmerman (Business Aligner)
Patrick Deroost (Podium)
Michael Poelmans (BNP Paribas Fortis)
Erno Spoelman (Gartner)
Marc Neyrinck (Add Business)

We can all agree that the rise in globalisation, the evolution in technology and the Internet have changed the way organisations compete and manage their customers. Globalisation triggered many organisations to look for mergers and acquisitions in order to improve their global reach. New technologies and the Internet enabled organisations to acquire and manage their customer through the Internet and call centres even questioning the need for a sales force in the future.

In our high streets we notice how small retailers are being replaced by big global corporations. In the business to business environment it means that many suppliers have to compete globally for fewer but much larger customers. The increase rate of competition and change means that organizations find it increasingly more difficult to keep innovating their products and services. As a result many products are becoming commodities making price the most important factor to compete on. The largest pain for most sales organisations is to keep finding ways of adding value with the fear of being replaced by an Internet portal or a Call Centre.

But, what if there was a way that sales forces can help their organisation stay ahead of the competition and innovate? Many organisations we interviewed in our research find ways to do just that. Would you like to know how they did that and how they are preparing themselves for the future?

Meet SteelCore (pseudonym) a steel manufacturer operating in an industry which is highly commoditised. One of their business units develops critical steel components for the car manufacturing industry. Confronted with a rising competition from other countries offering low cost alternatives they are pressured to innovate and come up with new ideas if they want to survive. Their new innovative products have recently ended in failures as their customer showed no interest in them. They realized they could no longer continue to innovate by themselves so they started involving their customers in the process. By co-creating new products with their customers they not only increased their business relationships with these customers but this also provided them with the new innovations they needed to address in their larger market.

As a result they have been able to develop new innovative products one of which became a block buster product afterwards. This approach enabled them to use their sales force as a strategic tool to develop new products and build new collaborative relationships with customers making it very difficult for their competitors.

Throughout the book we have included many more examples of how organisations are finding ways to use their sales force to build and sustain their competitive advantage. These examples and findings are based on a research project we started 2010 in collaboration with the **TiasNimbas Business School, Cranfield University** and the **Sales Management Association in the Netherlands**. The aim of the project was to identify current and future trends in sales. Over a period of 2 years we have interviewed well over a 100 senior sales executives from industry, academia, sales consultancy firms and representatives from sales associations across the US, UK and central Europe. We targeted organisations with a field sales force of minimum 100 people. In addition, sectors where well documented transformations have occurred were targeted to conduct the study. For instance, the pharmaceutical sector was particularly relevant to illustrate the profound changes this industry is experiencing as a result of regulation in health care. Information systems and engineering solutions are appropriate contexts to illustrate the challenges of complex selling; fast moving consumer goods (FMCG) companies were selected to gain insights from a key sector in developed economies, often highly concentrated and in many instances strongly driven by price. Professional and financial services provided evidence of sales transformations in contexts where solution and relationship selling are perceived to be critical.

Besides studying these trends we also helped many organisations to transform their existing sales force allowing them to stay current. We call this transformation "From Selling to Co-Creation" and to help you achieve your transformation we have included in this book cases, tools and framework to use in your own organisation.

Chapter 1
FROM PAST TO FUTURE COMMERCIAL TRENDS

PAST
TRENDS

CURRENT
TRENDS

FUTURE
TRENDS

PAST TRENDS

Before looking in the current and future trends in sales it is useful to remind ourselves about what were the prevailing views at the end of the last century and see how selling and sales management evolved from there.

During the 1990s, we witnessed the rise of the relationship era whereby organisations were building long-term, satisfying relations with their customers in order to retain their loyalty when buying their products. The central notion was that the cost of attracting a new customer was estimated to be five times the cost of keeping a current customer happy. This trend was fuelled by market deregulation, free trade, democracy and capitalism all giving rise to market globalisation. As a result, some organisations became larger and global through mergers and international expansions. In industrial markets, sales processes became increas-ingly shaped by fewer, larger and more powerful purchasing organisations.

This era also saw the rise of software applications such as Enterprise Resource Planning (ERP) and Customer Relationship Management (CRM) systems, together with the Internet. These offered opportunities to introduce a more fact-based form of sales management. The principles emerged from the manufacturing industry and focused on understanding the cause and effect relationships between processes and their outcomes. This approach to management relies largely on fact-based quantitative measures and benchmarking methods. In a sales environment this implied that all sales processes had to be broken down into separate distinct phases, for accurate analysis. Each stage included a specific set of sales activities that ensured a business opportunity matured from a 'lead' to a 'closed deal'. The

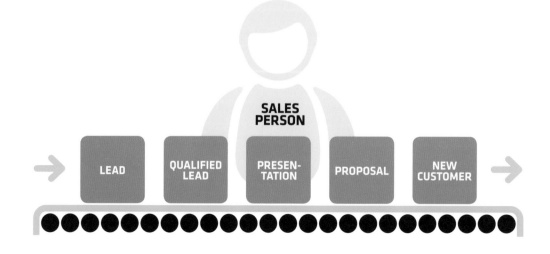

SALES PERSON

LEAD → QUALIFIED LEAD → PRESEN-TATION → PROPOSAL → NEW CUSTOMER

NUMBER OF OPPORTUNITIES

DURATION OF OPPORTUNITIES

CONVERSION RATIO OF OPPORTUNITIES

REVENUE ESTIMATE OF EACH OPPORTUNITY

measuring and benchmarking of these activities amongst sales people led them to adopt statistical process control approaches.

Using statistical process control charts, sales managers can determine what the quality norms are for each stage of the sales process. These conversion ratios express the amount of leads and opportunities that are abandoned during each stage of the process and which are considered normal. This is often represented by a sales funnel.

Funnel management consists of constantly comparing sales people's ratios with those that are considered the norm, and investigating the causes where they deviate. It is argued that this approach enables a sales manager to detect problems related to selling skills and to time and territory management. Low conversion ratios would reflect selling skills problems, and unbalanced amounts of opportunities at each stage would reflect time and territory management problems. This relies on a command and control management approach whereby in exchange for pay, sales people give up autonomy permitting their managers to direct their work activities and to monitor their performance. In such a management approach sales people are considered rational human beings primarily motivated by pay.

The rapid evolution in technology give rise to e-commerce allowing organisations to bypass their sales channels and sell their products directly to their end users. As sales channels disappeared, many suggested that the internet may be the end of the traditional sales force. 'Sales force effectiveness' became 'sales effectiveness' given that selling no longer required a physical sales force.

Of course, in 2010 when we started this research, we knew sales forces had not disappeared. If anything, they had become more important in creating business growth. This motivated us to go out and interview sales executives to hear about the main trends they saw, the challenges they had been dealing with in the last 10 years and how they saw the future of their sales organizations.

CURRENT TRENDS

When conducting the research, we identified four major trends that are impacting sales organisations. The first is the continuing effects of globalisation. The second trend is the on-going effect the Internet has on the buying behaviour of customers. The third trend is the growing importance of efficiency within the modern sales force. The fourth trend is the growing importance of ethics and the compliance with new laws and regulations in the contexts within which sales organisations operate. These trends have been changing the landscape of sales greatly over the past ten years. We now look at each of these together providing some illustrative examples.

GLOBALISATION

Market globalisation as a trend already started in the 90's and even continues to affect the way organisations do business today. As a result, organisations become larger and global, through mergers and international expansion. For the sales organisation, globalisation means fewer but larger customers, but also a centralisation of the purchasing effort and a rationalisation in the number of suppliers. The reason for the reduction in suppliers is to increase buying power and to achieve further price reduction selecting a smaller number of suppliers. As a result, a very large proportion of a suppliers' overall revenue stream is generated by a very small number of customers. How do suppliers manage this increasing reliance on fewer customers?

A distributor of professional printing equipment reported that their customer base had shrunk from 1,600 professional printers to 250 over a period of approximately 10 years. Some companies went bankrupt or stopped trading but most of them consolidated into larger groups. As a result, they are now doing business with fewer but much larger customers

creating a whole new set of challenges. These, now large customers wanted to use their buying power to their advantage and sought to deal directly with the manufacturers. In the past, manufacturers were reluctant to engage straightforwardly with end users because they did not have the logistical facilities to service these customers. However, with fewer customers, the requirements in terms of logistics are strongly reduced. By cutting out the intermediary, the manufacturer can split the commission otherwise paid to the intermediary with the customer in the form of price reduction and use the rest to handle the logistical costs. As a result, the reseller invested in new added value services. One of their main strengths as opposed to the manufacturers was their knowledge of the full printing processes. By offering additional products and services, they are able to differentiate themselves from the manufacturer as a supplier of solutions rather than of machines (i.e. products). To manage these larger customers the sales force has been restructured replacing the territory based sales force by key account managers. The revenue amount generated by their larger customer means that losing one customer is decisive in reaching the organisation's sales targets. Therefore, they responded to this situation by implementing strategic account management procedures and teams within their organisations. As part of the transition, they asked their account managers to interview their customers on how they saw the future and used that information to guide their internal strategic reorganisation exercise. As a result, this organisation transformed from being a product-oriented towards a customer-centric organisation. By working much more closely with their customers, they are able to better manage their dependency on their customers but also to discover new ways to continue to add value. Suppliers rely increasingly on fewer but larger customers referred to as strategic customers. Losing such a customer can mean for many organisations

that the looses may not be compensated by the number of new customers it acquired during that year. As a response, sales organisations introduced new sales roles such as Key Account Management and Business Development Management. These sales people in these new roles, manage large amounts of revenues and often lead a team of people to coordinate all commercial activities necessary to manage their accounts. They are typically people who can nurture long-term customer relationships by becoming trusted advisors for their accounts and by demonstrating a solution-driven focus. They are in charge of sales, customer satisfaction and ultimately profitability and customer value. The revenue size of such customers for many sales organisations we interviewed became so large that sales suddenly became a boardroom topic, including directors and general managers in the composition of the key account team.

MANUFACTURER
PRESSURE

SALES FORCE

CUSTOMER
PRESSURE

PAST
TRENDS

CURRENT
TRENDS

FUTURE
TRENDS

INTERNET

The internet has greatly empowered customers making it much more difficult for suppliers to add value to the sales process. As a result, customers are more involved in the purchasing process and have become much more demanding on their suppliers. They want to ensure that what they purchase will actually increase their competitive advantage.

Because they are much more informed they have much less need for face to face contact with a sales person. The Internet has effectively become the source of knowledge for customers. As result the role of the sales person as an information provider is disappearing. This raises the question: How can a sales force reinvent itself in order to remain relevant to its customers?

According to one large international financial institution, their customers in the past showed little involvement in the decision of which products and services they needed. They trusted their banks blindly and were more willing to accept the ways of working of their bank. Today through the Internet customers are much more knowledgeable about the bank's products and services. The industry has been pushing for more product transparency, which made it easier to compare products and services between different banks. As a result banking customers these days are more involved in the choice of the products and services they want. In addition, they expect high quality, 24/7 service. These new requirements cannot be met through generalist sales people working out of branches operating with strict opening hours. As a result, the bank restructured its sales channel by reducing the number of branches and providing their services through the Internet and call centres. However, these channels have their limitations, which created the need for highly specialised sales forces that add value by analysing the customer's needs and recommending the most appropriate financial services solutions. These specialised sales people operate from home and are able to meet the customer at a time and place of their convenience. As a result, the effectiveness of the sales force has greatly increased as they are now able to provide their customers with expert in-depth advice.

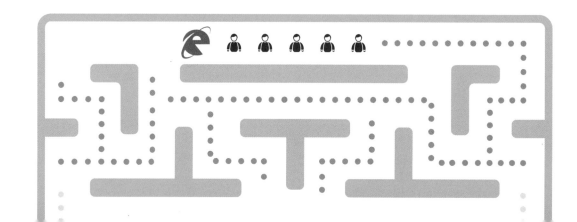

Developing personal relationships with customers has in the past been the synonym for adding value. Being product centred does not mean organisations cannot provide added value to their customer. As one sales manager from this financial institution told us "our customers do not want a relationship they want expert advice".

Over the last 10 years sales forces consisting of generalists have been struggling to add value to their customers and they have been replaced, where possible, by lower cost channels such as call centres, self-service portals or through smaller local resellers. Nevertheless, there is still a substantial amount of customers who need more in-depth assistance. Sales forces are still required but they need to be highly specialised in order to add value to their customers. We believe that sales managers should be more critical about whether the so-called relationships their sales people have with their customers really add any value.

EFFICIENCY

Globalisation also brought more pressure on the sellers' margins. In order to remain profitable, many organisations have to constantly reduce their sales forces while maintaining sales revenue targets. On the one hand, organisations have to reduce the number of sales people and on the other hand they have to build better relationships with their large customers. So, how do sales forces build close relationships with their customers while on the other hand reducing their size?

One way consists of visiting customers less frequently. One sales manager in the steel manufacturing industry showed how the number of sales people had almost reduced a ten-fold while his sales targets remain unchanged. When asked how they can combine this reduction in resources and the need to build better and more professional relationships he answered: "Our customers are faced with the same reduction of resources and have less time to meet up with suppliers. As a result we see our customers less but when we see them we need to make an impact." Another sales manager disclosed the results of their customer satisfaction survey in which customers revealed that their sales people were calling on them too often without a meaningful reason. The speed at which people rotate jobs in many organisations also makes it very difficult for sales people to build personal relationships.

These examples show how difficult it has become for sales people to develop long-lasting personal relationships based on frequent contacts. These days, account management is no longer about building personal relation-

PAST
TRENDS

CURRENT
TRENDS

FUTURE
TRENDS

ships but about building business relationships. These new forms of relationships are primarily built and maintained based on the added value provided by the supplier.

Another way organisations have been increasing their efficiency is by automating more of their internal work processes through Enterprise Resource Planning and Customer Relationship Management systems. These systems also play a large role in shaping the type of relationships sales people have with their customers. As one interviewee from a manufacturing organisation said "our sales people cannot get things done for their customers without following the rules and entering the data in the systems anymore. In the past, the sales people could go in the warehouse and make sure extra products were loaded on the truck for their customers. This is no longer possible which is very difficult for many of our older sales people to accept." For sales people this has meant that they are no longer able to develop personal relationships with their customers by 'fixing' things for them.

The changes in the way relationships are built with customers are often difficult to accept by sales people, particularly those who were used to build relationships via high levels of personal contact. Interviewees told us that the former generation of sales people typically viewed their role as someone who does personal favours and builds personal relationships in return for business from their customers. Today business

relationships are built on the added value the sales force can bring to the customer's business. This redefines the skills and knowledge that are required of sales.

ETHICS AND REGULATIONS

The rise of business ethics, corporate responsibility and, in some sectors the appearance of new legal regulations are forcing suppliers to review how they build relationships with their customers. The fear of negative media coverage and legal lawsuits has triggered organisations to formally define how its sales people must develop relationships with their customers.

Sales people have traditionally enjoyed a fair degree of autonomy. This has been justified by the fact that not all territories and customers are the same and that sales people must have the flexibility to adapt. This raises the question: how to adhere to regulations without infringing too much on the level of flexibility and autonomy the sales people need to be effective?

Several sales managers in the financial sector agreed that before 2000, their sales approach was based on what they called "hit and run". The consequences of the financial crisis and the fear of negative media coverage and law suits have prompted organisations to formally define how their sales people must develop relationships with their customers. In one instance, a sales manager told about a legal dispute her company was facing initiated by a customer who, after an accident, could no longer repay a mortgage. The customer claimed that the sales person did not fully explain the risks involved and the benefits of taking extra insurance for these types of incidents. This raises the question: how can you, as a sales person, claim you have given full information?

Over the past decade, the sales profession seems to have gained a very poor reputation which is not restricted to the financial sector. As a result, several sales organisations go a long way in structuring their sales approaches and systematically documenting their activities. To ensure customers could not be persuaded too quickly some financial institutions implemented new sales processes dictating that a customer must be visited at least twice before a deal could be signed, and each step of the process must be recorded in Customer Relationship Management systems (CRM). This, in itself, is not new. What is new is the fact that this financial institution also has its CRM data and sales approaches externally audited. As one sales manager told us, having a bad auditors' review with regards to implementing the sales process has severe consequences. These new rules are not limited to the financial sector. One electronics manufacturer told us that as a result of stricter compliance regulations they also implemented very formal rules on how to sell to their customers. Formally auditable

sales processes enables suppliers to formalise the sales process and to show that their sales people exercise "due diligence" when selling products and services.

Well-documented and audited sales processes do not mean that the customer is getting more and better information or service. So, how can we audit the customer experience after having met with a sales person? Many organisations we interviewed were measuring their customer satisfaction, some using one version or another of the Net Promoter Score method. One of the main advantages of this method is that it offers a way to measure satisfaction using only one question.

Taking advantage of this, some sales organisations have started measuring the satisfaction of their customers after they have spoken to one of their sales advisors. Customers are asked questions such as "You have recently had a meeting with one of our advisors. Would you, based on this meeting, recommend us to your family and friends?" Several financial institutions started using this method after the financial crisis in 2008 to ensure their advisors would no longer engage in any hard-selling activities. Some even used this as a performance indicator for their sales people.

Working in a more controlled sales environment also requires a specific type of sales person will-

PAST
TRENDS

CURRENT
TRENDS

FUTURE
TRENDS

ing to accept this new way of working. To that extent, many organisations have been adapting the profile of the sales people they recruit to fit better with the new analytical business-oriented sales person demanded by customers. This has also led to a shift in remuneration methods from sales commission on sales results towards a combination of fixed salary and bonuses. One European manufacturing organisation reported that their sales people have a high fixed salary and a relatively small yearly bonus. The system is setup by their HR department and is harmonised across the whole of the organisation. However, their reward system in Europe is different from the system they operate in the US and in Asia. The different reward structures are based on cultural differences but also based on legal constraints in the different countries, which limit the options of how to reward people. With the exception of a few organisations, which operate through self-employed agents, most sales managers are no longer considering the financial reward system as a means to motivate their sales force. As one sales manager from a German manufacturing organisation told us, "people seem more de-motivated by the fact they did not receive their bonus than they were motivated when they did receive it." There is an increasing belief that commission-based reward

systems promote a more operational mind-set with short-term thinking, which is the opposite of what most sales organisations expect from their sales force.

Several interviewees labelled these changes 'a move from an art' towards a profession whereby sales people have to follow rules and standards dictated by their organisation. Some viewed it as a loss in autonomy for the sales person, while others saw it as a professionalisation of the sales function, which will attract more analytical and business-oriented people to a career in sales. These people do not see these new more formalised processes as a loss in autonomy but as a structure helping them in their jobs. We discussed this trend in a seminar of a sales association, where one attendee commented "it looks as though we are taking the fun out of sales". We asked what the audience thought about it and we have been asking our audiences this question even since. While a very small minority agree that sales is less fun than it used to be, the majority of people still find the job very challenging.

PAST
TRENDS

CURRENT
TRENDS

FUTURE
TRENDS

FUTURE TRENDS

Interview data revealed five major trends that will likely affect the way sales forces will operate in the near future. The first trend is the growing importance that customers are going to play, in the development of new value propositions. The sales process, as we know it, will evolve into a co-creation process. The second trend concerns the need to develop and manage an ecosystem of partners which are needed to co-create new value propositions. The third trend is the growing importance of knowledge management in sales. Knowledge, and more specifically know-how, will become more important than products during the sales process. Capturing knowledge and disseminating it will be one of the main challenges for the sales force in the coming years. Social media will begin to play an ever more important role in helping the sales force to co-create, partner and manage knowledge. This is the fourth trend. The fifth trend is the switch from selling products or solutions to the actual business service rendered by these products. Outsourcing and managed services are already leading the way. These trends will result in the landscape of sales will continue to change greatly over the coming years. We will now look at each of these, illustrating with some examples from organisations that participated in the research.

CO-CREATION

In the past, innovation was something that happened only inside a supplier's organisation and which resulted in a product or service that the sales force could then sell. Now, however, there is a growing segment of customers which wants to be actively involved in the innovation process. They no longer wish to be passive recipients of products and services designed for them but they want to help in designing the products and services they use. This means engaging customers in co-creation, which is the process whereby all key stakeholders (customers, sellers and partners) collaborate in the development and the use of the products and services. For them the opportunity to participate in such a process is a great part of the value proposition itself. Developing new products has traditionally been the role of market-

ing. So, what if there is a way for the sales force to involve the customer in the development of new products?

One large multinational industrial organisation closed down their internal R&D department a couple of years ago. Their sales manager told us "Our market is very mature and our customers are very knowledgeable. We are no longer successful at developing new innovative products by ourselves anymore. As a result we have closed down our internal R&D department. New products will have to be developed together with customers under cost and revenue sharing agreements. Part of the role of our sales people is to find customers or prospects who are willing to collaborate on new product development projects."

This example shows how some organisations

are reversing this conventional path to profitability. Their logic is "we sell first and we will build it later". The "we" in this context involves the supplier but also the customer and other parties who are interested in the project. This new approach is made possible by the fact that their customers want to get involved in the design, production and the marketing of their value proposition. So much so that in countries where the company in question lacks production capabilities and hence does not offer the possibility of collaboration to their customer, they struggle with their sales performance. In other words, the option of co-developing new products is becoming a powerful part of the value proposition.

The industrial organisation completely reversed its commercial process. However, involving the customer in the development of new products does not come without its complications, as one equipment manufacturer experienced. To-

gether with several customers, they developed a new product to improve the weaving production process of their customers. The impact of the new product on the customer's business was so significant that the manufacturer quickly saw the commercial benefits. After introducing it into the market, sales rose immediately. As a result, the manufacturer decided to raise the price of the product. This led to a severe breakdown in the relationships between the manufacturer and the initial customers who participated in the development of the new product. What initially looked like a customised development project for a few customers, turned out to become a major technological innovation. The lack of rules and agreements on how to deal with such circumstances led to commercial problems. As a result, the manufacturer developed framework agreements to define what happens with regard to the intellectual property rights and how the commercial

PAST
TRENDS

CURRENT
TRENDS

FUTURE
TRENDS

benefits are to be divided.

We believe that co-creation of value propositions together with customers and partner networks will become a standard way of selling in the future. While currently such initiatives are only triggered on demand of the customer in the future sales people will have to become more proactive in offering such forms of collaboration. According to the interviewees, the act of co-creating new products with customers can be part of a Unique Selling Point (USP) that can help to attract prospects and improve customer relationships. The process is complex, so suppliers will have to develop guidelines to manage the co-creation process.

KNOWLEDGE AND CAPABILITY MANAGEMENT

For many sales people the changes mentioned so far mean they have to acquire much more business knowledge and sector knowledge, thus their role is evolving towards management consultants. The competitive advantage of a sales force in the future is likely to be less defined by its products and more by its knowledge. Therefore, knowledge management is an increasingly important aspect of the sales function, playing a crucial part in developing a competitive advantage.

The knowledge needed is no longer that from technical product brochures and descriptions. As one manager in a consulting organisation referred to, knowledge management is about generating new insights based on sales people's experiences and interactions with customers. This means that interaction be

tween customers and the sales force, becomes a mechanism through which new insights and knowledge is generated. The challenge for many sales managers will be to find ways to capture and replicate this knowledge. This raises the question: How can sales managers capture and share knowledge within their sales organisations? Through storing and sharing their information, through teamwork, through job rotations and through workshops with customers.

INFORMATION SYSTEMS AND KNOWLEDGE SHARING

One business consulting organisation showed us its knowledge management system and explained how they use it in combination with a series of internal meetings to ensure best practices and information are shared. Its system is managed by dedicated people who make sure that after the completion of a project all the team members submit their information and key learning points from the project. While this information is valuable, the tool in itself is not enough to ensure that their senior consultants and partners have all the knowledge they need. For that reason they organise once every two months a full day event which they called "college days", where they focus on learning about one specific topic. Twice a year they organise formal best practice exchange meetings. On top of that, they organise sector meetings to exchange knowledge and information related to project within a specific sector on a regular basis. In their view, the key is not only to capture and store the information but also to ensure the information is shared.

TEAMWORK

Teamwork has become a common approach in selling. One manufacturing organisation started to actively encourage their sales people to participate in product innovation projects. These projects consist of a sales person, a technical advisor, and a marketing manager. Their goals are to create and sell new applications for their existing technology. These projects not only lead to innovations and market penetrations but also allow the sales people to network within the organisation and increase their overall knowledge.

JOB ROTATION

Another practice to facilitate knowledge management came from a sales manager in the logistical sector who introduced a system whereby all new sales people must also work part-time in its operations department for a limited period.

CUSTOMER WORKSHOPS

All these examples show how sales organisations are implementing new ways to share and exchange as much information internally as possible. However, sales people can also exchange knowledge with customers and partners. To that extent, the key account managers of a large system integrator organise, once a year, a workshop for each of their top customers which is called "Customer Experience Journey". These are two-day workshops, which both the customer and the supplier's teams attend. The aim is to exchange information about their goals and how they can help each other to achieve them. Interestingly, the focus is not only on how the supplier's team can help the customer achieve their goals but also vice versa. According to them, these workshops are very useful and have produced many different solutions to help improve relationships. They also proved to be a valuable source of information to develop key account plans.

These examples illustrate that sales managers do not believe that learning and knowledge acquisition can be achieved through systems alone. Instead, it must include a culture process that values the exchange of best practices internally and externally with customers and partners.

We believe that sales people will no longer be able to rely on the superiority of physical products and production facilities as a means to maintain a competitive advantage. Their true source of competitive advantage will be their knowledge and especially "know-how". Organisations will need to define their co-creation processes and identifying the knowledge required to engage in these processes.

PAST
TRENDS

CURRENT
TRENDS

FUTURE
TRENDS

PARTNERSHIPS AND NETWORKING

Both customers and suppliers are actively involved in establishing partnerships with other organisations in order to co-develop solutions. As both customers and suppliers have their own networks of partners, sales people need to coordinate the activities of their own network with those of their customers. How to manage these networks, or ecosystems, is, for both customers and suppliers, a relatively new process. "This process is much more difficult than one might expect", an executive from one global system integrator reported. As part of the globalisation process, his company saw its customers reducing the number of IT suppliers to a number of four to five. While the consolidation of suppliers increases the customer's buying power, it also creates a new challenge. In order to keep their suppliers committed to the relationship, they need to balance the amount and type of work they assign to each of them. They do this by assigning projects to each supplier based on what they perceive to be the supplier's core strengths: Innovator, process specialist, low cost, local player, etc. One problem associated with this approach is that suppliers are expected to stay within the category (the tier or segment) the customer placed them in. When suppliers start competing with each other and trying to become more important for the customer, they are making the customer's task of managing the supplier ecosystem very difficult. As a result, our research showed several customers stopped working with some of their main suppliers because these suppliers did not want to behave in a way consistent to the tier they were assigned to. Another difficulty is that customers expect their suppliers to work together. The suppliers are partners when serving one customer but competitors when pursuing another. Thus, sales people have to manage how much information they are willing to share with other suppliers in one project knowing that this information may be used against them in another project with another customer. Interviewees revealed that they share all the information that is relevant to complete the project at hand. It is recognised that the main source of competitive advantage is the know-how or in other words the capability organisations can develop based on this information.

Like the conductor of an orchestra, sales people are moving into a role of coordinator of activities between a complex ecosystem of customers and partners.

The sales process is moving away from selling standard products and services to the co-creation of value propositions with customers and partners. The sales person's value propositions are based on capabilities, which need to complement with the capabilities of the customer and its partners in order to create and deliver the required solution. This calls for suppliers to identify which core capabilities they have in house and which ones they need to source via partners in order to build specific solutions. Networking becomes an important activity to bring together the components needed in the creation of a total value proposition for the customer.

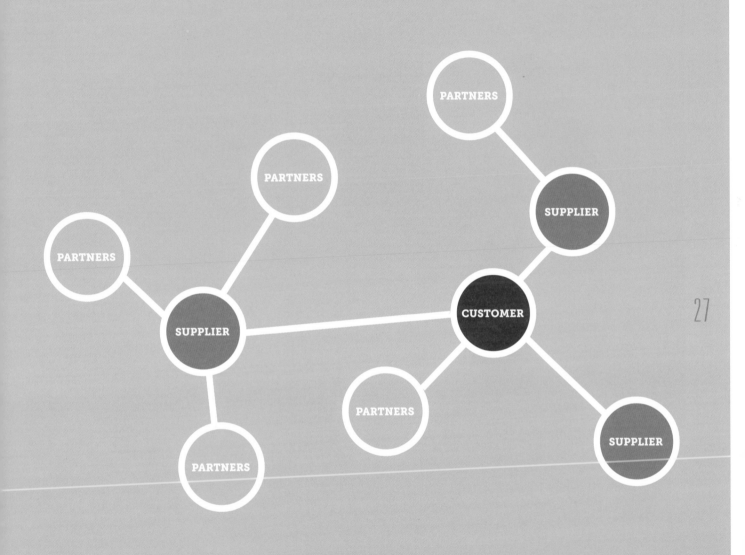

SOCIAL MEDIA

The Internet and social media have brought about opportunities to streamline the communication processes with transactional customers. Internet-related technologies and applications can increase efficiency but also can improve the customer experience. Interviewees reported that until now they have looked to the internet and social media as means to reduce their costs whereas in the coming years these tools and means of communication will become the norm and they will have to embrace them as an integral part of customer management and communication strategies. Can social media facilitate both efficient customer processes and increase customer experience?

The business banking division of a financial institution might have an answer. They saw an opportunity to build a community connecting their small to medium business-to-business customer segments. This bank identified that executives often seek the advice of personal coaches and people who can act as a sounding board to give them valuable feedback. In large organisations management consultants fulfil this role. In smaller organisations with small training budgets, executives have the need but not the luxury. How could they obtain external advice? They came up with a solution to this question through a business portal. When talking to their customers they noticed that while many seek advice, others are very willing to offer their advice and experience. The business portal acts as a market place for those who seek advice to find those who are willing to give advice. The bank developed the portal at its expense. The benefits for the bank are based on the belief that when customers help each other to make good business decisions it will lead to more business investments at a lower risk, thus indirectly improving the business of the bank. The success depends on the bank's ability to keep the portal interesting enough for their customers to return to and to ensure the portal becomes a helpful resource in helping its users grow their businesses.

This approach, of developing a portal to connect customers together offers other commercial advantages. By having customers advising each other, organisations may be convinced to do more business or to make more investment in their own business. Whenever it is they need financial support in the future, they will likely turn to the partner who helped them in the first place. By offering and promoting the opportunity for their customers to interact with each other, the bank is also enabling relationship building and this may increase their loyalty to the bank.

Portals such as these can also be of value to sales people. Because not all customers will use these portals, sales people can act as brokers on their behalf. If a customer needs some marketing advice they can use the portal to find some other customer who might be able to help them. This example shows how social media platforms can help sales people add more value to their customers using the possibilities offered by the internet and social media.

In a networked economy the products and services that a sales person can sell are being replaced by 'capabilities' that allow them to co-create solutions with their customers. In this example, social media provides sales people with a whole new set of capabilities which they can use to grow their sales helping customers in indirect but valuable ways.

The principle of leveraging the capabilities of your partners, suppliers and customers does not actually require any social media technology. Many sales organisations already do this through networking events, which they organise for customers and partners. Social media provides a cost efficient way to this but perhaps more importantly, in our view, it is creating a mind-set where this sort of innovative thinking and opportunity exploitation becomes the norm.

PAST
TRENDS

CURRENT
TRENDS

FUTURE
TRENDS

FROM PRODUCT TO SERVICES

Globalisation and the Internet have greatly impacted both customers and suppliers. Suppliers have suddenly found themselves competing with organisations around the world, increasing the pressure on price and quality. Customers who once relied on local suppliers to inform them about market and product evolutions, have found themselves empowered with knowledge, choice and the ability to easily compare the quality and the price of their value propositions. In many industries, suppliers find themselves competing with an increasing amount of players that offer better quality at lower prices. How can suppliers compete in markets where their products are constantly outperformed by their competitors in quality and/or price? We found several organisations who managed to outperform their competitors by moving away from competing on the product and focussing on the services, sometimes delivering a totally different offering.

For one IT system integrator the increasing amount of new competitors created a serious problem. Developing highly customised solutions led them, over the years, to handle a great variety of different technologies and products. This meant high internal costs to maintain all these technologies and products. Lack of local competition allowed them, overtime, to charge a premium price for their services. Rising international competition meant that customers could find support for their technologies at a cheaper price and at a better quality. By focusing too much on providing highly customised solutions and less on selling replicated solutions they found themselves unable to compete. As a result, the organisation decided to drastically reduce their product and technology portfolio in order to minimise their internal support costs and to increase their levels of service quality. By focusing on offering managed services solutions they convinced their customers to outsource the maintenance of their IT system to them. This meant that customers would no longer have to worry about which technology they used as long as it provided the business benefits they required. By no longer having to support all these different technologies they were able to reduce their costs and invest in increasing the quality of service. For the sales people this meant their sales message was no longer 'technical' but 'business-oriented' in nature. Since other businesses can also offer these types of services, they also need to explain why their services will have more value to their custom- ers. This also requires them to have an in-depth knowledge of their customers operations. As their sales manager said "our sales people need to learn how to help our customers to manage operational expenditure budgets." This example shows how the role of the sales force is shifting from selling products or services towards ensuring that the customer does obtain the maximum value from the ser- vices and products offered.

Offering managed services also open new possibilities to add value to your custom- ers. Rolls-Royce, the British manufacturer of aircraft engines, created new ways to combine products and services[1]. Instead of just selling their engines, Rolls-Royce offers its custom- ers a more flexible option known as "power by the hour®" where the customer pays according to the utilisation of the engines. This requires Rolls-Royce to engage in a close relationship with its customers for the alignment of their mutual processes. The investment in engine- related services has led Rolls-Royce to develop other capabilities such as engine monitoring ca- pabilities. This enables the company to track in

real time the performance of engines in opera- tion and to schedule repair and maintenance in a planned manner. Rolls-Royce can even offer the service of training pilots to optimise engine performance in flight operations. This form of close collaboration delivers value for both Rolls- Royce and its customers. These customers are no longer buying a product but a service, which is delivered by the product.

These examples illustrate that from the point of view of the customers, value is only cre- ated when using the product. In other words, customers may not be interested in the product but in the benefits they can obtain from using it. This means that the sales process is not fin- ished once the contract is signed. Sales people need to ensure their customers actually obtain maximum benefit from the products and the services they sell.

The role of the sales person is changing from selling the product or service to selling the value delivered by the bundle of product/ service. This change of focus may allow a sales person to compete in markets where they may not be selling at the cheapest price. For the sales organisation, it means that their sales funnels are getting longer! What used to be the domain of customers service is now part of the sales process.

Chapter 2
FROM THE OLD TO THE NEW COMMERCIAL LOGIC

WHAT IS THE NEW COMMERCIAL LOGIC?

THE OLD COMMERCIAL LOGIC

1. Gain market knowledge about customers wants and needs;

2. Design and produce new value propositions to meet these needs.

3. Contact customers and prospects to sell new value propositions.

THE NEW COMMERCIAL LOGIC

1. Contact customers and prospects to co-create new value propositions.

2. Design and produce new value propositions to meet these needs.

3. Gain market knowledge about who else may have the same wants and needs for these value propositions.

The approach to manage large sales forces that dominated the last decade of last century, emphasised maximising efficiency. Generalist sales representatives were deployed into territories and into functions often characterised as 'hunting' and 'farming'. The primary function of the generalist sales person was to persuade, inform and assist the customers to complete their purchases. In today's business environment, activities such as order processing are better performed by lower cost channels, such as, self-service online portals and call centres. So, a key question to reflect on is what will be role of the sales force tomorrow?

The same market forces that are driving sales forces to be replaced are also creating new opportunities for sales forces to add value. Globalisation, leading to fewer but bigger customers, means that suppliers are exposed to a much greater risk. Losing one large customer might have significant financial repercussions. As a result, organisations are actively redeploying their sales people to manage these accounts. The focus is gradually changing towards smaller but more effective sales teams whereby knowledge and expertise, not just tasks and activities, is the main principle for sales force design.

The speed of change in the market also makes sustainable innovations very difficult and to continue to add value for their customers organisations have to take higher levels of risk. Also, in todays' environments conventional methods of market research take too long and cost too much to deliver insights that will lead to real innovations, those that customer will appreciate and buy. In business markets, customers often want to be involved in the design and development of the products and services that they need. This offers the opportunity for suppliers to design and develop new products together with their customers. Co-creation therefore means that suppliers are able to share innovation risk with their customers. As a result, organisations are redeploying their sales people to manage their key customers and to contribute to co-create new innovative value propositions. In doing so, they are effectively changing the logic of how organisations develop and commercialise their products and services. In the old commercial logic marketing would, through focus groups or other market research techniques, gather information about the needs and wants of their customers. These are then translated into new products or services, which after being produced are sold by the sales force. In the new commercial logic the sales force is used to manage key customers and to co-create new products and services with them. After they are produced, marketing looks for ways to commercialise them further to a broader market.

This is not about downplaying the importance that marketing will play in the future versus sales in B2B contexts. This evolution of the role of marketing is in line with recent debates about how to deploy marketing and sales to maximise their joint effectiveness. The evolution in the marketplace is witnessing how deep business relationships are becoming the most important tool in a supplier's commercial toolset. Establishing these relationships is important not only from a commercial risk perspective, but also because they are vital to provide the basis for product and service innovation. The sales force is the most appropriate resource to manage these relationships and to facilitate and sustain innovation processes. Marketing techniques such as campaign management are more appropriate to commercialise and distribute these new innovations in the wider market.

Implementing this new commercial logic will, for most organisations, require a lot of changes to their existing sales forces. So, let us have a closer look into the implications this has on the sales force concerning:

- **What type of sales people we will need in the future?**
- **What type of sales processes we will have in the future**
- **What type of sales organization design we will have in the future?**
- **What type of sales management approach we will need to adopt in the future?**

WHAT ARE THE IMPLICATIONS FOR THE SALES FUNCTION?

The spectrum of the traditional sales process is expanding to cover the full gamut of the customer buying process. From helping the customer to define their strategy to helping the customer identify their problems and solutions, to helping them use their products and services to their maximal potential[1].

FROM PAST TO CURRENT

The nature of selling in many sectors has evolved from 'persuasion' towards 'advice'. In order to add more value to selected customers sales organisations have advanced their transactional tactics into a consultative sales approach. Self-service portals and call centres enable customers to purchase directly, reducing the need for transactional sales people. Overall, customers require their sales people to have much more knowledge about their own products and services as well as about their customers in order for them to add value. This has led to the creation of selling teams that combine different types of expertise to help their customers to identify their problems and propose the appropriate solution. This approach is often labelled consultative selling, because sales people are focused on helping customers to see how the seller's products and services can solve some of the their problems. This approach became very popular over the past

decade for two reasons: Firstly, it enables sales people to add value to their customers during the sales process. Secondly, the earlier the sales person is involved in the customer's buying process the more they may be able to influence the buying criteria in their favour.

FROM CURRENT TO FUTURE

The move towards consultative selling has been one of the responses to the fact that customers no longer see value in sales people who are only able to talk about the features and advantages of their products and services. Today's sales people need to help customers see how their products and services will benefit and will have a clear positive impact onto their business. These benefits are tightly linked to the problems the customer is experiencing. As organisations are also becoming knowledgeable about their problems and needs, sales people will yet again have to upgrade their approach to continue to add value. In the future, sales people will have to become like 'business consultants' offering strategic advice while also offering advice on how to extract a maximum value from using the vendor's products and services. This means that in the future customers may no longer be interested in building relationships with suppliers whose added value is largely limited to matching their products and services to the customer's needs. Customers will want to work with suppliers who can help them in (re)defining and implementing their strategies or plans. This implies that customers will have to involve their key suppliers to make their strategic or business plans for the coming periods. For system integrators (e.g. automotive, aerospace) for instance this means that the production and operations managers will become interfaces with key suppliers and will have to involve them when defining their respective strategies and plans. For management consultants it means that the boards of directors may wish to involve them when defining their business strategies. When the strategy or plans are articulated, the customer may also expect its suppliers to help in the implementation of these strategies. This means that the suppliers must ensure that the products and services they sold do actually enable the customer to achieve their goals. The shift towards consultative selling implies a fundamental transformation in the type of knowledge and skills sales people will require in the future. It also requires redefining the scope and nature of sales methodologies and processes.

CUSTOMER'S BUYING PROCESS ⟩ STRATEGY ⟩ ROADMAP ⟩ PROBLEM ⟩ SOLUTION ⟩ SUPPLIER ⟩ PURCHASE ⟩ USE ⟩

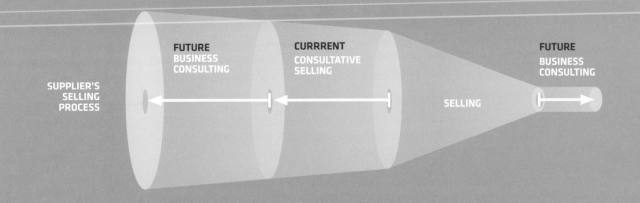

SUPPLIER'S SELLING PROCESS

FUTURE BUSINESS CONSULTING

CURRRENT CONSULTATIVE SELLING

SELLING

FUTURE BUSINESS CONSULTING

WHAT ARE THE IMPLICATIONS ON THE SALES PROCESS?

From a sales process perspective, we could conceptualise the evolution of selling as a move from helping the customer to solve their problems to helping the customer to identify and implement new possibilities for taking their business forward. This requires a substantial rethink of some of the sales processes and methods used today by sales forces around the world. The trends in selling and sales management call for a paradigm shift from "selling to customers" towards "selling with customers". What this means is that helping the customer to identify and to define and to implement new business possibilities requires the customer and the sales person to act as partners, engaged in processes of co-creation. When co-creating business possibilities, the customer and the sales person decide together which solutions they need to support the realisation of the customer's future plans. During this process the core capabilities of the supplier are no longer their products and services but their capabilities to identify, define and implement business solutions. A sales process which is based on capabilities and which involves the customer in some form of co-creation is a relatively new phenomenon and process for many organisations. Without a proper methodology and relevant systems in place, this approach may only be adopted by supplier-customer dyads that have a vision of how to use it for their joint advantage. For customers not willing to engage in co-creation, suppliers need to consider formalise and optimise their sales methods in order to manage non-core customers in a sustainable way.

THE IMPACT ON THE COST OF SALES

The co-creation sales approach implies longer and more complex sales cycles. Sales organisations need highly educated sales people to act as consultants and such an approach means higher sales costs. This poses a financial dilemma for organisations that may be facing decreasing margins as a result of intense competition. One large financial institution decided to offer an added value service providing advice to their customers as part of their relationship approach to banking. The advice was not product-related but was about helping their customers to plan and manage their financial future (i.e. "financial planning"). While their research showed that their customers valued their advice, it was also revealed that their customers were price conscious. At that time, the cost of the advice was included in the fees customers were paying for the bank's services. After the banking crisis of 2008, however, they were obliged to show the commission amounts that were being paid for the advice to their customers. This led to the question, if given the choice, would their customers want the advice and would they be prepared to pay for it? Knowing their customers they were convinced that they would not be prepared to pay for such advice. As a result, they chose to adopt a product-centric approach adding value by offering in-depth product knowledge and expert advice to their customers without any additional service.

This example illustrates how important it is that the customers are prepared to pay for extra (or value added) services such as advice if the seller is to run a sustainable business. This is an essential consideration in defining the sales strategy and process. The extent, to which additional services are perceived as valuable, has implications in terms of how a sales force provides value to their customers. If the customer refuses to pay for value added services, then the role of advisors (as opposed to product specialists) when selling financial services needs to be reconsidered.

There is agreement however, that in many other contexts (specialist technical functions) the expertise and insight of professional sellers is appreciated and highly valued by customers. Some of the organisations in our research were investigating ways in which they could monetise (i.e. invoice) their customers for the account managers' time spent in customer engagements. If customers require their supplier's sales people act as business consultant or advisors, arguably they should be prepared to pay for that advice. After all, consultants do charge their customers for their time and advice so why not sales people who adopt a consultative selling approach? The argument we often hear is that the price of the sales person's advice is included in the price of the supplier's products and services. Customers are often not used to pay for the advice they receive from their supplier's sales people so why make it all more difficult than it already is? One reason is that in order for your advice to be accepted by your customer it needs to be credible and unbiased.

This is the case for one large photocopier product manufacturer. Having developed a full range of products, and managed services solutions, they observed that many of their customers relied on external advice from consultants when choosing and selecting investments in technology. They decided to set-up a consulting practice and hired consultants to go and help their customers. Because they manufactured these products worldwide themselves, they would have an edge in terms of knowledge and competencies over other local independent consultants. To their surprise, customers were not interested in their services. At first, the customers were reluctant to accept that the manufacturer was able to provide business-consulting services. Some customers questioned whether the advice would be objective and independent. This case company eventually succeeded in overcoming these problems but not without difficulties. At the time of conducting our interviews, they were bidding for a large consulting assignment whereby they would also have to manage and work with the products of their largest competitor. This required a complete new mind-set whereby they now also offer solutions, which included servicing products they do not produce themselves and for which they get paid separately.

This case provides an example of how embarking in genuine consultative selling is far from easy, the extensive investment required to train sales people to become truly 'consultative sellers' and the new mind-set and organisational culture that underpin solution selling.

WHAT ARE THE IMPLICATIONS FOR THE **SALES PEOPLE?**

In traditional 'hard selling', the sales person explains the product or service and expects the customer to be able to match the product features to the benefits of addressing their needs with that product. In consultative selling, the sales person first helps the customer to identify their needs before presenting their products and services. Still, both approaches are rooted in a product-centric view. A customer-centric approach involves looking at the problem from the customer's perspective. This requires the seller to be unbiased and to advise the customer what is best for them. In many cases, the ideal solution for the customer may be to integrate products and services from several other vendors. This brings to mind a famous quote from the former CEO of IBM, Louis Gerstner, who said that the only way to see whether you are really customer centric is when you recommend your competitors' products[2]. However, the approach also needs to be profitable for the seller. This requires the seller to have a relatively large portfolio of products and services, which can be integrated in many different ways. The scope of the product range and the ability to integrate these products in different ways offer the possibility to create highly customised solutions, which is an essential dimension for a customer-centric approach.

Being customer versus product centric requires a very different mind-set. The customer-centric mind-set starts from the ambition of finding the best solution for their customers. Their targets include customer profits or customer share of wallet (i.e. the percentage of a customer's expenses for a product that goes to the firm selling the product). The product-centric mind-set starts from the ambition of convincing their customers that their products are the best solution for them. Their sales targets include product-based revenues and margins.

Moving from a product towards a customer mind-set is difficult. It requires sales people to change deeply held assumptions and beliefs about how to best sell to their customers. The sales cycles are much longer, more complex and, more importantly, the sales people do not fully control the process. The lack of control over the process and the uncertainty of the outcome makes it much more difficult than selling off-the-shelf products. For these reasons it is extremely difficult to change a sales person from a product towards a customer mind-set and it is virtually impossible to have one sales person doing both. Many sales managers we encounter believe that the lack of customer centricity among their sales people stems from a lack of skills. They believe that customer centricity can be achieved through training and coaching. This is a over simplification of the problem. If we want sales people to change their view about their job, we have to redesign the jobs, which mean redesigning the sales organisation.

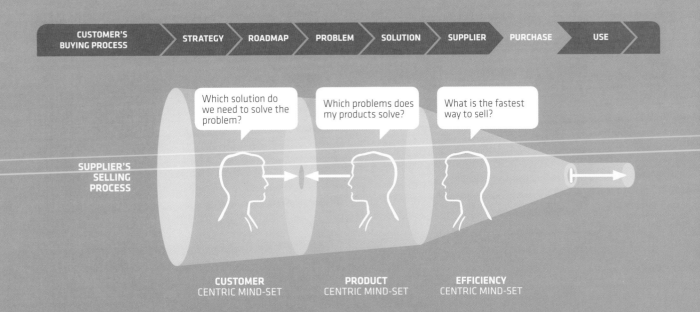

WHAT ARE THE IMPLICATIONS ON THE DESIGN OF THE SALES FORCE?

MARKETING　　　　**SALES**　　　　**SERVICE**

The functional organisation whereby marketing, sales and customer service are separate departments is based on the notion that the customers are part of one single market segment all following the logic of a single commercial process. This is no longer the case for many organisations. The change in purchasing power has forced suppliers to adopt different approaches for different customer segments making the old functional organisation model for marketing, sales and customer service no longer appropriate. As one interviewee claimed, the changes required to co-create value and implement a customer centric culture do not impact solely on the sales organisation, they have a wider impact on the whole organisation. These days, customers require more added value through customisation and collaboration in the design and development of their products and services. By opening up organisations and inviting customers to collaborate, you no longer have control over the sales process. The sales process becomes a sales co-creation process, unique to every customer.

Today processes such as key account management and business development management no longer fit the standardised, traditional and linear sales processes. In addition, the amount of knowledge and know-how required to add value to the customers, requires more teamwork and collaboration between all the customer-facing departments.

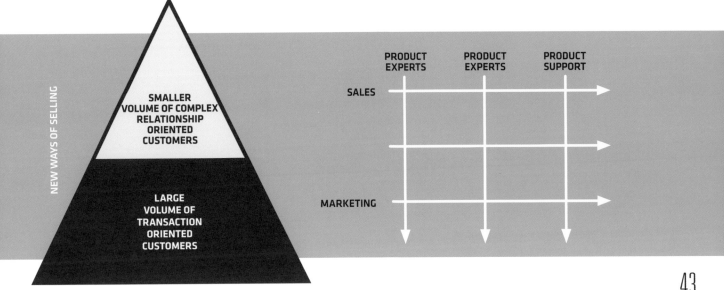

SMALLER VOLUME OF COMPLEX RELATIONSHIP ORIENTED CUSTOMERS

LARGE VOLUME OF TRANSACTION ORIENTED CUSTOMERS

PRODUCT EXPERTS   PRODUCT EXPERTS   PRODUCT SUPPORT

SALES

MARKETING

43

To co-ordinate all activities, one person or department needs to be made accountable for managing the commercial process. Therefore, organisations have been segmenting their customers and allocating strategic customers to individual account managers and other customers to marketing departments. Both also receive the authority needed to command resources they need to manage their processes. This has led to many commercial organisations adopting a matrix structure. The matrix structure not only allows you to combine knowledge and know how required to manage customers it also allows organisations to combine different mind-sets and selling approaches. The matrix enables customer-centric sales people to manage individual accounts while calling upon the help of product specialist sales people who work within different product units. From a customer's perspective, it also enables the customer to choose their counterpart depending on what type of advice they want from their supplier. For instance, when a customer wants business or more strategic advice they may contact their account manager. However, sometimes they also just want to buy a particular product and only require some technical advice. Then they can contact the product sales person directly. The key difficulty for the supplier is to ensure that all these customer contacts somehow do not lead to internal conflicts, which may harm the overall relationship with the customer.

IBM
FRONT BACK
ORGANISATION

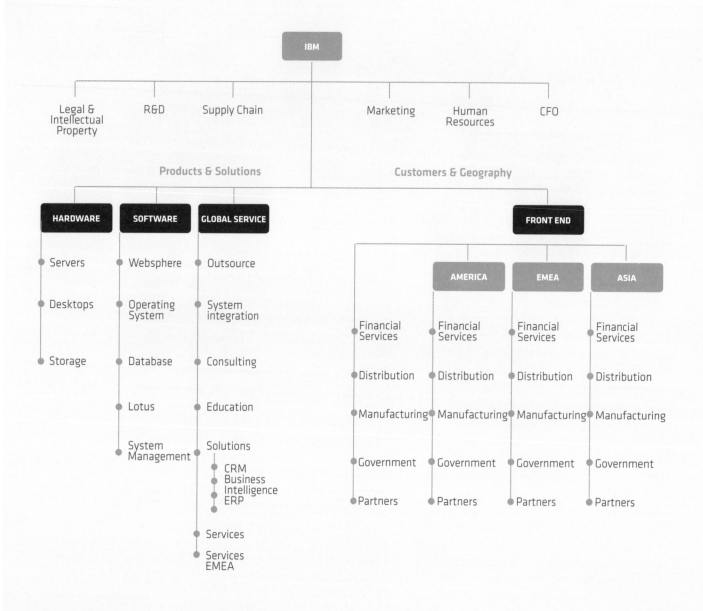

One well-known case was the turnaround of IBM, which went through a major reorganisation of the type described above under Lou Gerstner's leadership from 1993 to 1998[2]. He believed that customers wanted a supplier who could both create technologies and also integrate them. This gave rise to a new form of organisation known today as the front-back organisation. This form of organisation consists of multiple business units whereby some operate in the front-end and develop solutions with customers, and the back-end, which creates products and services to be used as building blocks for the solutions.

The sales people in the front develop customer relationships and organise all customer-facing activities. This requires both project management competencies as well as in-depth customer knowledge. Customers are typically served through relationship managers with a deep understanding of the customer and their industry.

The sales people in the back sell and promote their products either by selling them directly or by collaborating with their colleagues in the front units. This requires selling competencies as well as in-depth-product knowledge.

In our research, we realised that there were some major cultural issues arising from separating customer from product-related sales forces. These sales forces require different types of sales people, different processes and different reward systems. This can lead to some internal conflict: a product-oriented seller (e.g. someone who sells servers) at IBM is seen to be on the side of the seller; however, the outsourcing and consulting sales people from IBM may suggest a Hewlett-Packard server if it makes more sense for the customer. In order to maintain credibility with the customer, the people from the customer-centric business must not be biased towards IBM equipment when the organisation is engaged in configuring and selling a total solution. They must be on the side of the customer in the buyer-seller transaction. Such discrepant mindsets may inevitably lead to internal conflicts.

To solve these conflicts and to channel them to create positive outcomes, procedures need to exist so that various different sales roles and many different types of sales people can co-exist under the same organisation.

HOW TO DECIDE WHICH SALES STRUCTURE IS BEST FOR YOUR SALES ORGANISATION?

Being a customer centric organisation has become such a fashion that the label 'product centric' organisation is perceived negatively. This raises the question whether all organisations have to be customer centric to be successful.

According to Jay Galbraith , an organisation can only really be customer centric if it is able to provide custom-tailored solutions[3]. This ability is defined by the scale and scope of the products and services offered and the degree of integration of these products and services. Scale and scope refer to the number and kind of products that are combined into a solution. The degree of integration refers to the ability and the need to integrate these products and services into customised solutions. These days many organisations seek to become customer centric making product centric something no organisation wants to be labelled as. In our view the important element in the model is that building a customer centric organisation is based on an organisation's ability to build custom solutions for their customers. To achieve that, organisations need a wide variety of products and services that can be assembled in many different ways to suit particular needs. This does not mean that organisations with few products do not value their customers or their customer's opinion. It also does not mean that their products are offering a solution to their customer. What it does mean is that the solution offered cannot be tailored to the specific needs of each individual customer. We need a product centric organisation that can develop state of the art products and services as well as a customer centric organisation that can develop tailor made solutions to solve specific customer problems.

Based on a simple questionnaire an organisation can easily measure the extent to which it can truly be said to be customer centric. Select which of the following statements best describe your organisation's value propositions in terms of scale and scope and level of integration. By taking the sum of both values corresponding to the selected statement you can identify which level of customer centricity is best for your organisation on the customer centricity radar.

46

HOW TO DECIDE WHICH STRUCTURE YOU NEED?

SCALE AND SCOPE

1. My company has two to five similar products or services to sell to the same customer.
2. We offer five to ten mostly products and services.
3. We have ten to fifteen products or services of different types to sell to the same customer.
4. We have fifteen to twenty variegated products or services to sell to the same customer.
5. We have more than twenty products or services of various different types to sell to the same customer.

INTEGRATION

1. My company provides stand along products to the same customer with common invoice and billing ("one-stop shopping")
2. My company has a set of minimally connected stand-alone products (like a common brand, common experience, combined shipment)
3. My company has minimally packaged (themed) components that need to work together for customer segments
4. We have modular components of products and services that need to work tightly together as a system.
5. We have very tightly integrated packages/bundles/full solutions of products and services to offer to customers.

Source: Jay R. Galbraith, 2011, Designing the Customer-Centric Organization, John Wiley & Sons

SONY PROFESSIONAL SOLUTIONS EUROPE
A PRODUCT CENTRIC SALES ORGANISATION

A total score, on both questions, of three or less suggests the organisation will benefit more from adopting a low level of customer centricity. Such levels include the product-centric approach, whereby voluntary collaboration between the units are allowed but not structurally promoted.

For years, Sony Europe's sales organisation was organised by country. Each country managed its own profit and loss accounts and had to sell the entire product line in its own region. The product line included the following categories: media and broadcasting, security, medical devices, display, printing, and solutions. The product categories differ not only by products but also by distribution channels and margins. Each country had the autonomy to define their strategy in order to achieve a set financial target. As a result, most countries focused more on certain product categories than on others. Sony's reputation and market share in media and broadcasting has been traditionally strong. In order to reach their revenue and profit targets, country managers focused on those products, which were most likely to generate the amount of sales. Sony felt it was losing out in some new markets. They needed to find a way to ensure all of their product categories received sufficient sales attention. One approach could have been to change the rewarding system. Sony did not believe this

would solve their problem. To resell and service the whole product range requires a substantial amount of expertise and resources. Depending on the size of market for some countries, the investment in resources would not be justified. As a result, Sony changed the design of its European sales organisation from local sales organisations (selling the total portfolio of B2B products) with their own local profit and loss accounts and strategy to vertical business units dedicated to one product category.

The benefits for Sony were:
1. Greater focus on the product category;
2. in-depth knowledge of the industry/market;
3. from sales generalists to sales specialists;
4. harmonised strategy and approach of the market (making it easier to address Pan European customers);
5. faster decision-making and implementation across all the countries; and
6. clear accountability.

After one year of experience in the new structure, the Security Business Unit identified that their different customer segments could be served even better by having more specialised sales positions aligned with those customer segments. On top of their product specialisations, they further divided their team into customer specialists implementing a two-tier model (Distributors – Resellers and finally end user) with three types of sales teams:

1. Distribution account management: focus on transactional selling, channel marketing and managing all the process management between Sony and the distributors.

2. Channel account management: manages a portfolio of second tier resellers, to educate, advise, and support in joint visits to end-users.

3. Business development management: team dedicated to demand creation by approaching key end users in the vertical market segments that Sony identified as being strategic. They have to play a role of evangelist, prescribing the products to end users and consultants. They are the door openers for the second tier resellers who will make the actual sales to users and consultants. They are the door opener for our 2nd tier resellers who will do the actual sales.

This case illustrates how organisations are moving away from a generalist sales force due to a lack of added value these sales forces can provide to their customers across the whole product line. Sony's decision to move towards a product centric sales organisation was based on the fact that their product ranges service very different markets and purposes. Their resellers on the other hand provide Sony's customers with solutions for their specific problems. In their product portfolio Sony is only one of their products, which they use to build solutions. In effect, the combination of product vendors such as Sony and resellers does lead to a matrix of different sales organisations working together to assemble a tailor made solution to their customers.

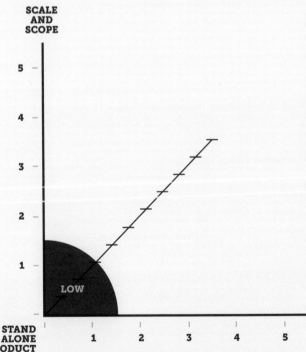

RICOH
HIGH CUSTOMER CENTRIC

A total score of seven or higher suggests the organisation will benefit from adopting a strong level of customer centricity. At this level, the customer dimensions are reaching strategic importance to the level of the product units. This level leads towards a matrix organisation whereby customer and product sales units are equally important in the go to market process. In some cases, customers may even become so strategic that separate units are created and dedicated to specific customers. These units combine resources from different locations, products and markets into specific units.

Ricoh is a global provider of technology to enable transformation in business processes and that provides solutions for document and information management. Ricoh aims to help businesses become more productive and profitable. Over recent years and through a series of strategic acquisitions, they have positioned themselves to become a service-oriented company, providing end-to-end solutions through their expertise in their four core capabilities: Managed Document Services, Production Printing, Office Solutions and IT Services.

The sales force is organised in a matrix structure. The vertical dimension consists of the individual product and solutions business lines. Each of the business lines have their own profit and loss account and have their own sales force to promote and sell their particular product or solution. The horizontal dimension consists of client managers, who are focused on selling and servicing customers across all the product lines.

The role of the client manager is that of an account ambassador. For their customers their role is that of a trusted advisor and for Ricoh their role is that of an opportunity spotter. They are rarely fully involved in selling campaigns. The objective is to detect or create business opportunities and pass them on to the sales people in the respective business lines. The sales people in the different business lines perform the actual selling and bidding. They have the knowledge and they have the responsibility for the profitability of their own business lines. As an ambassador, the key account manager can influence these activities but has no formal authority over them. Once a relationship has been established between the sales person from a vertical business line and the customer they may be involved in sales transactions without needing to involve the client manager.

This case illustrates how the role of the account manager is mainly one of facilitating the collaboration between the customer and the supplier. The complexity of managing large customers shows how this role is taking precedence over other traditional sales activities such as bidding and managing price negotiations. Releasing the account manager from the tasks of creating proposals and formal price negotiations, allows them to remain a neutral party focussing on keeping all parties collaborating. This does not come without its challenges. Having no say in price negotiations may create the perception of irrelevance in the eyes of the customer and in the eyes of fellow colleagues in the different product units. The account manager therefore needs to demonstrate high levels of business knowledge and be recognised as a valuable advisor to both his/her customer and his/her internal colleagues. Failure to do so will lead to the account manager being seen as irrelevant.

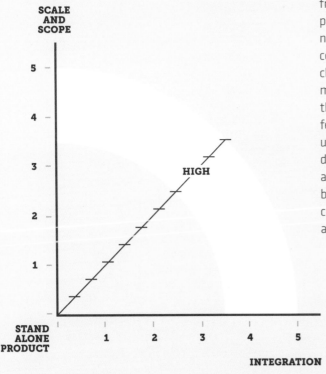

WHAT ARE THE IMPLICATIONS ON THE SALES MANAGEMENT FUNCTION?

Henry Chesbrough , professor at Haas Business School in Berkley, who coined the term 'open innovation', uses the concept of a funnel in the sales process to represent the life cycle of innovation ideas towards marketable products[4]. He argues that traditional organizations' innovation processes were closed, which meant they did not include partners and customers. Open innovation on the other hand includes customers and partners but with the consequence that the innovation process is no longer following controlled processes like that of the funnel. He represents the funnel as one with a hole where opportunities leave and come back at later stages. His point is that once you open up to collaboration you no longer have full control over the innovation process. Sales executives are often trained to 'control the process' as part of their training and job definitions, which is in sharp contrast with the reality of the market dynamics in many sectors. This leads us to the question whether sales funnels as a tool to manage customer acquisition, to calculate conversion rates and to evaluate the sales force are still relevant.

While funnel management may offer some value in terms of forecasting, opportunity management is more appropriate. In a key account management context, each opportunity and each customer are unique and need to be assessed and managed according to specific circumstances. With account managers, we notice they have must less control over the individual processes and more control over the overall customer context. The control shifts from process to relationship. The concept is still widely used but evaluating the sales force using indicators such as conversion ratios is no longer relevant.

For one large international bank, we conducted a study analysing its funnel data. The objective was to see whether a correlation could be established between their data and the motivation, skill and knowledge levels of their account managers. The bank was hoping to use these correlations to benchmark their account managers with each other. Not only did we not find any correlations, but also we noticed unusual patterns with the data, which at first looked like data quality issues. For instance, many opportunities were being reported in the CRM system the same day or several days after the contract was signed with the customer. When we investigated it further we found that many account managers experienced difficulties in reporting precisely the stages at which their opportunities were. Therefore when they were required to input the opportunities in the system they relied on guessing and intuition. Having so many interactions with their customers it was not always clear, if and when an opportunity started and when it was closed. This was an issue their colleagues focussing on acquiring new customers did not have. As a result, a sales manager in this bank preferred coaching and steering their sales

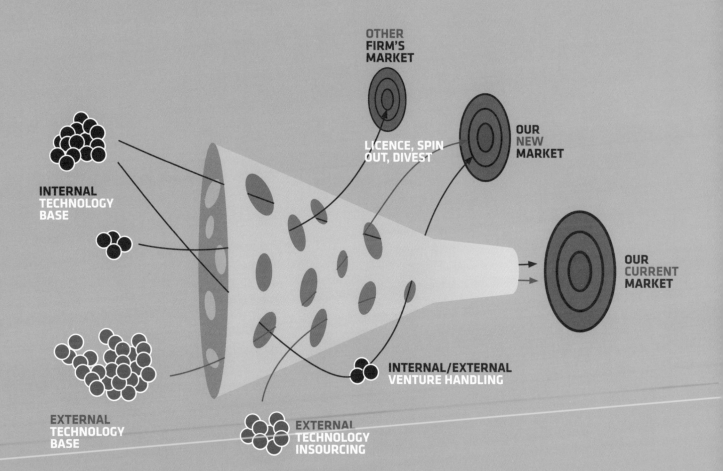

OTHER
FIRM'S
MARKET

OUR
NEW
MARKET

LICENCE, SPIN
OUT, DIVEST

OUR
CURRENT
MARKET

INTERNAL
TECHNOLOGY
BASE

INTERNAL/EXTERNAL
VENTURE HANDLING

EXTERNAL
TECHNOLOGY
BASE

EXTERNAL
TECHNOLOGY
INSOURCING

Henry Chesbrough, 2003, Open innovation: The new imperative for creating and profiting from technology, Harvard Business Press

people based on each individual opportunity rather than on some (questionable) statistical benchmarking report.

WHAT SHOULD WE MANAGE?

With fewer but bigger customers to manage, the value of an organisation becomes increasingly defined by the relationships it has with its customers. In other words, customers are one of the organization's most important assets. We argue that the people managing these high value assets are not sales people but business managers. Senior sales leaders therefore need to focus on how account managers create customer value and on how well are they able to enlist the support of other team members, to collaborate towards the end delivery for the customer. When managing large accounts, account managers often have to make decisions which impacts beyond the traditional fiscal year period. For that reason their performance needs to be evaluated taking into account the lifetime value of the customer they manage. Managing key accounts also requires key account managers to obtain the collaboration of internal resources over which they often have no formal authority. This process of making sales people accountable for achieving an objective relies on the underlying notion of the "controllability principle" whereby the sales person is able to control how he or she will achieve his/her objective. This raises the question: How should the management approach be adapted in order to account for the fact that the achievement of individual objectives requires teamwork?

Based on the traditional view where a link must exist between accountability and controllability, individual objectives should not be assigned where teamwork is required to achieve this objective. Accountability without controllability conflicts with established organisational theory and is considered to create dysfunctional outcomes and job-related tensions and stress. Nevertheless, most sales force these days (and is an increasing trend) rely on teams of people working together to manage and to develop relationships with their key accounts. One way to solve this dilemma is to design the organisation in such a fashion that everyone is dependent on each other in order to achieve their targets. This inter-dependability encourages the development of reciprocal understandings, arrangements and obligations that make cooperation both desirable and necessary.

We are witnessing that many activities of traditional sales forces are being replaced by co-creation type of activities focusing not just on business outcomes (e.g. closing deals) but on creating value for the customer and for the supplier. Not surprisingly, the metrics used to measure sales performance are also evolving towards measuring the profitability and value of each customer for the supplier. Sales management activities are therefore also shifting from monitoring and coaching individual sales behaviours, to monitoring and facilitating collaboration and team work between sales people and all other employees involved in managing customer relationships. Sales management activities are therefore also shifting from monitoring and coaching individual sales behaviours to monitoring and facilitating collaboration and team work between sales people and all other employees involved in managing customer relationships.

SUMMARY

In this chapter we have argued that new business models, some stemming from open innovation, some form the service dominant logic, and some from entrepreneurship are finding their way into the heart of marketing and sales organisations. Out-dated approaches for new venture creation involved a lot of market and desk research in order to write a detailed and complete business plan including three to five year's financial projections. Based on this plan funding was raised in order to develop the products or services completely before launching them in the market. According to Steve Blank this old approach is the reason why 75% of all start up's fail[5]. Instead, entrepreneurs are encouraged nowadays to regard their ideas are merely hypotheses that need to be tested as quickly as possible. This market hypothesis must be tested using the minimal amount of product development possible and by involving customers and partners as early on in the development process as possible. Once tested, entrepreneurs are encouraged to pivot on the original idea in order to improve their ideas when going to market.

The new commercial logic suggests that the role of the sales person is evolving towards that of an entrepreneur and that large customers are becoming the organisation's innovation partners. Based on the success of innovations tailor made for one or a few customers, marketers can pivot on the idea in order to turn it into a successful value propositions appealing to a wider market. The skill sets for co-creating are based on the ability to develop deep customer relationships in combination with good business acumen and leadership.

In the following chapters we will dive deeper into these issues by addressing each of the following questions:

1. How to progress from Selling to Co-creating?
2. How to progress from Customer to Asset management?
3. How to progress from managing to collaborating?
4. How to change sales people's perception of their work from job to calling?

Chapter 3
FROM SELLING TO CO-CREATING

WHAT IS CO-CREATION?

The rate of change and innovation means that organisations can no longer rely on their physical infrastructures and products to sustain their competitive advantage. Instead, organisations need to rely on their knowledge and capabilities as their main source of competitive advantage. Firstly, an organisation's competitive advantage today is largely dependent on its ability to understand subtle mechanisms to create value and to create the systems to make that creation work. Knowledge and especially know-how, which is the application of knowledge, is increasingly the source of competitive advantage. Secondly, the focus is shifting from delivering value propositions towards helping the customer to create value. This is the shift in focus for the sales force from distributing products manufactured by the organisation towards delivering a service to their customers. Stephen Vargo, marketing professor at the University of Hawaii, and Robert Lusch, marketing professor at the University of Arizona describe this shift as the shift from "Goods Dominant Logic" towards "Service Dominant Logic"[1]. In the goods dominant logic the sales person's focus is to sell a 'good' to a customer and it is up to the customer to ensure they get the expected value out of it. In the service-dominant logic the sales person focus is to ensure the customer get the value they need through the use of their products and services in particular ways that may be different from customer to customer. Vargo and Lusch use the singular term "service", indicating a process of doing something for someone, rather than the plural "services", which are another form of goods, which are sold to customers. In other words, products are becoming a means to an end, which is to assist the customer in getting the value they are looking for. This is best illustrated by the quote of Theodor Levitt "People don't want a drill, they want a quarter of inch hole". The good or product is the drill; the service is to drill the hole where, when and how the customer wants it and the value is the hole itself. So, instead of selling drills, how can sales people collaborate with their customers to ensure they get the hole they want? This does not necessarily mean we should stop selling drills and drill the hole on behalf for our customers. It means that selling the drill is no longer your main goal. Your goal is to ensure the customers get the holes they want. At first, this does not look surprising but when you start analysing it, it has fundamental implications for the role of the sales force.

Let us stick to the example of the drill. First, what the sales person sells is no longer state of the art drilling equipment. The value proposition is helping the customer to get the job done as well as possible. For that, the sales person's knowledge and know how is about the job to be done by the customer and not about features and advantages of his or her drilling equipment. Second, the sales process is not about persuading the customer to buy your drill. The process is about understanding the customer's job to be done and deciding on the best way to do it. This understanding may suggest that the best approach is buying a drill (the traditional option, the one offered by traditional sellers), but others may include hiring a contractor to do the drilling, selling a drilling service etc. What is important is not 'what' or 'how' you sell it but instead how you collaborate with the customer to ensure the best option to get the job is done well is selected, irrespective of how or who does the actual job. The experience of both the sales person and the customer are important in a service-dominant logic approach. The experience can be viewed as the final outcome, who did what, what knowledge did they get out of it and how did it make them feel. Did the customer get what they were after? Did the customer get involved in the process? Did the customer learn something out of the process? How does the customer feel about it? These elements will determine whether the customer will continue to work with us in the future and hence increase their lifetime value for us. In this example, value for the customer is co-created by the interaction between the customer and the sales person concerning the job the customer wants done. This means that the customer is always involved at in the process, learns something out of the process and has a feeling or emotion about the whole process, thus both tangible and intangible outcomes may be created, both tangible and intangible forms of value.

In this process, the experience of the sales person (as well as the customer's) is important. The first reason is that the sales person also needs to learn something out of the process. This learning is vital because it adds up to the knowledge and know-how of the sales force. In other words, it enhances the total value proposition, which is based on organisational capabilities, business relationships and of course, product/service attributes. The second reason is that the satisfaction or dissatisfaction of the sales professional with the process may impact his/her level of intrinsic motivation. Sales people who fully engage in the customer co-creation process often do so because they feel positively challenged by this approach and feel motivated by its pursuit. If the sales person is not motivated or enthused they may eventually fall back to 'selling drilling equipment' by focussing on the features and advantages of their products, which is their traditional comfort and control area. In other words, they behave consistent with the goods dominant logic and see their role as one of distributing their organisation's products or services.

Before going into more detail about the co-creation process let us first, define what we mean by co-creating. Since co-creation is all about value, we must define what we understand by the term 'value'. There are many definitions of customer value but the best definition so far is the one by Christian Grönroos, marketing professor at the Hanken School of Economics in Finland, who defines value for a customer as[2] :

"Value for customers means that after they have been assisted by a self-service process (cooking meal or withdrawing cash from an ATM) or a full-service process (eating out at a restaurant or withdrawing cash over the counter in a bank) they are or feel better off than before."

This definition points out that value is created by the customer and is based on their experience in using a product or service. Value is not automatically derived from the product or service, but created with the product or service and based on the customer's user experience. In the co-creation process, suppliers and customers are mutually engaged in the development of the product and services they use. Value is created by involving customers in the supplier's design and production processes and by involving the suppliers in the customer's usage processes. In this process, resources of both the supplier and the customer are combined creating new sets of capabilities. This enables both parties to achieve something that they could not have achieved alone. This leads us to define co-creation as:

"Co-creation is about transforming the customer in an active participant to be able to deliver him/her maximum value."

The co-creation process and the engagement of the customer is built upon four key principles . Understanding these principles is crucial to make the transition from selling to co-creating. These principles are:

PRINCIPLE 1
Focus on ends
instead of
means

PRINCIPLE 2
Turn your
customer into
an active
partner

PRINCIPLE 3
Develop value
propositions based
on organisational
capabilities.

PRINCIPLE 4
Focus on learning
through dialogues
and building
relationships.

PRINCIPLE 1
FOCUS ON ENDS INSTEAD OF MEANS

In the sales approach, suppliers and customers have discrete roles of production and consumption. Suppliers create products or services, which contain value and sell these to their customers. The perception of value creation is that it happens inside supplier's organisation through the supplier's own activities. In this view, the sales person provides value to their customers by selling them a product or a service. This is also referred to as value-in-exchange.

In the co-creation approach, the customer ultimately defines the value of a supplier's goods and services. The customer perceives and assesses the value based on their total experience dealing with the supplier and using their goods and services to perform the job they need to do. By this notion, value is created during the usage phase of the supplier's goods and services. For sales people to add value to their customer they must remain actively involved up until the moment where the customers achieve their desired outcomes (by using the supplied product / service). This is not the traditional moment when someone can say the deal is closed! On the contrary, the co-creation approach implies a much longer sales cycle, which requires that:

1. The sales people focus on customer experience rather than customer satisfaction.

2. The sales people needs knowledge about the customer business processes rather than product knowledge.

3. The whole organisation becomes customer-centric rather than product-centric.

CUSTOMER EXPERIENCE VERSUS CUSTOMER SATISFACTION

In the sales approach, the customer plays the role of information provider and user of the supplier's products and services. To ensure that customers are being well served and thus remain loyal, they are asked about their levels of satisfaction using a variety of means. The belief is that satisfied customers will not switch suppliers and therefore will remain loyal. Customer satisfaction can be seen as a measure of how well the supplier's products and services met or even exceeded the customer's expectations.

In the co-creation approach, the aim is to create excellent customer experiences. Customer experience is created through customer involvement, learning and perception of the outcome of the process. Experiences are not just about meeting expectations. They are about creating an emotion or a feeling about the supplier, the supplier's representatives and the supplier's products and services. An important driver in customer experience is the customer's ability to reach their desired outcome using the supplier's product and services. Even if the supplier's product or service met the customer's expectation if it did not enable the customer to reach their desired outcome it will not deliver a positive experience. This has important implications for the sales person's knowledge and skills. It requires them to understand what the customer is trying to achieve and to help the customer to define how they will achieve it. This also means that sometimes the sales person will have to challenge or even contradict the customer when there are discrepancies in perception about mechanisms to create value.

CUSTOMER PROCESS KNOWLEDGE VERSUS PRODUCT KNOWLEDGE

Most sales methods stress the importance of adding value by aligning all the key stakeholders at the customer end and by helping them to uncover their needs and make the best decision. This sales approach is largely focused on closing the deal. Once the deal is closed, it is out of the funnel and passed on to customer service. This is when a critical part of the whole

This approach leads to two problems. The first problem relates to the mind-set such approach generates. Sales people will inevitably focus on their part of the sales process and not on the entire customer journey and the customer's total experience. The second problem is that it limits the ability of the sales people to learn and to develop new capabilities. Convincing customers to engage in any form of co-creation requires a great deal of trust, which requires credibility from the part of the sales person. Such credibility is obtained by showing deep knowledge and know-how of the customer processes and the impact that the supplier

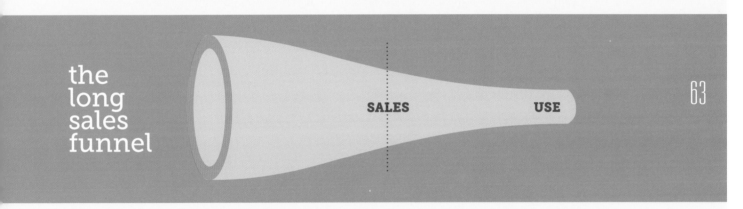

the long sales funnel

SALES   USE

customer journey starts, when the customer will determine whether or not they can achieve their outcomes. While some parts of the customer experience are determined during the sales process, most of the value is created during the usage stage. One could argue that from a customer's perspective, it is not important who from the supplier's organisation helps them to achieve their outcomes. It does not have to be the same person; it could also be someone else from a service department.

solution has on the customer organisation. This knowledge is created through the process of helping the customer to achieve their desired outcomes. By dividing the process, organisations often make it extremely hard for the sales people to accumulate the knowledge and experience needed to provide end-to-end services that lead to a superior experience. Tomorrow's sales people need process knowledge more than product or service knowledge. The sales person must acquire deep knowledge about the customer's jobs to be done, the problems the customers are experiencing when doing their job and how to solve them. They do not need to be able to solve the problems themselves but they need the know-how of how it should or could be done, engaging the required resources from their own organisation and often from their partners or the networks of partners.

CUSTOMER-CENTRIC VERSUS A PRODUCT-CENTRIC ORGANISATION

One cannot expect sales people to become customer-centric while the rest of the organization remains product focused. Adopting a co-creation approach is not something that can be limited to the sales department alone. It requires close collaboration with other departments to help customers achieving their outcomes. It is important to stress that it is not a sales trick. Organisational processes such as strategy and organisational design must be aligned with the customer-centric approach of the sales organisation.

PRINCIPLE 2
TURN THE CUSTOMER INTO AN ACTIVE PARTNER

In the sales approach, suppliers tend to view customers as adversaries, who they must persuade to buy their offer. Consultative selling and solution selling methods helped introduce the notion that in order to persuade customers you have to learn about their problems and needs through the means of a two-way dialogue. In order to define the solution for the customer, the customer must engage in the process by providing the information needed by the sales person. While this could be labelled as a form of co-creation, it reduces the role of the customer in the process to that of an informant. Furthermore, the customer is the recipient of the supplier's goods and services. In other words, the customer is 'sold to' as opposed to 'sold with'.

In the co-creation approach, customers have the opportunity to participate in each stage of the product or service production process. Consequently, this requires deep customer involvement in the supplier's service design processes where strong customer relationships are essential. In a co-creation approach, both the supplier and the customer are partners, engaged in a long-term relationship sustained by continuous dialogue. Considering customers not merely as informants but as active partners implies conceiving new customer engagement and relationship building processes that are based on co-creation instead of on traditional selling.

THE CO-CREATION PROCESS VERSUS THE SALES PROCESS

A sales process typically consists of a number of stages such as information gathering, proposal design, development of the value proposition and implementation the value proposition. Let us look at each stage of a sales and buying process and see how different they are when selling versus co-creating.

Information Gathering

In the **sales approach**, the sales person follows well-crafted interview methods that enable them to uncover the problems and needs of their customers. In the **co-creation approach**, the sales person and the customer have an open dialogue on how they could help each other to co-create solutions not just to pressing current problems but also to exploit future opportunities or to create future scenarios.

Solution Design

In the **sales approach**, the sales person matches the customer's needs to their products and services. In the **co-creation approach**, the sales person and the customer analyse their information together and co-define the appropriate solution.

Solutions Development

In the **sales approach**, the sales person negotiates the contract with the customer and the delivery team configures and installs the value proposition according to the pre-specified contractual agreements. In the **co-creation approach**, the supplier and the customer develop and implement the solution together sharing risks and benefits associated with the execution of the solution.

Installation and Use

In a **sales approach**, after configuration and installation of the product or service the customer service department becomes the main contact point for the customer. If the customer has a question, they can contact the supplier to get help. This service can be labelled as reactive!

In a **co-creation approach**, the development of the solution is not considered completed after the product or service is configured and installed: it does not end until the customer is able to achieve their desired outcomes. Helping the customer to use the value proposition to its maximum benefit is the most important part of the value proposition development. The supplier remains proactive during the whole process!

PRINCIPLE 3
DEVELOP VALUE PROPOSITIONS BASED ON ORGANISATIONAL CAPABILITIES

In the sales approach, the sales person's objective is to sell their products and services. They employ sales methods to identify the customer needs and link these with the features of their offering. In this context, solutions consist of different combinations of standard products and services.

In the co-creation approach, the sales person does not present the organisation's value propositions but instead presents its capabilities. From there, both the seller and the customer investigate how these capabilities could help the customer to improve its performance or to deliver its mission better. The focus is on how to share resources and capabilities to jointly develop solutions that will help the customer to do their 'job'. The sales person's products and services are the means to help the customer to create value and not the end themselves. In this context, the supplier's know-how, partners and skills are equally important parts of the value proposition. We make a distinction between knowledge, which is information, and know-how, which refer to organisational capabilities such as designing an IT infrastructure and bookkeeping. Know-how is based on knowledge but also on the ability to translate that knowledge into a process that will create value. Know-how is often the organisation's real source of competitive advantage. Approaching customers based on organisational capabilities rather than on individual products or services requires a different sales method that is focussed on a dialogue about the customer's job-to-be-done rather than the sellers' needs and wants. In the sales approach, the sales method is focussed on identifying the customer wants and needs. In the co-creation approach, the sales method is focussed around identifying what the supplier and the customer can do together. It is not about "what do you need" but "what can we do together". Typically, the nature of the dialogue that characterizes this approach is a very open ended one which may scare many sales people feeling the conversation becomes unfocused. For that reason the sales person needs focus on building a good understanding of the customer's job to be done, so the conversation remains structured and focused on a meaningful purpose. The aim is to uncover areas where both the customer and the sales person can collaborate.

PRINCIPLE 4
FOCUS ON LEARNING THROUGH DIALOGUES AND BUILDING RELATIONSHIPS

In the traditional sales approach, the more a sales person visits their customers the more chances they have to sell. The rationale is that frequent sales calls ensure that the supplier does not miss any opportunity to sell their products and services when the need arises within the customer. Through these interactions, the customer learns about the sales person's products and services and the sales person learns about the customer's problems and needs. Both use that information to select the most appropriate strategy to interact with each other. The learning is limited to improving the efficiency of existing processes.

In the co-creation approach, interactions are part of dialogues between the sales people and their customers. As opposed to a semi-structured interview, a dialogue consists of a two-way communication. In a co-creation approach, the dialogues are centred on the various issues, which relate to the job the customer has to do and their experiences resulting from doing their job. This includes dialogues about the customer's customers; trends and evolutions in the market that affects their job and their own customers and the outcomes of certain solutions to name just a few. The learning happens through the exchange of information and feedback allowing both the supplier and the customer to learn about new issues but also to consider adapting their internal processes. The learning is not about improving the efficiency of some processes but about changing existing or developing new organisational practices. In our research, all the organisations we analysed that adopted in some way the co-creation approach, showed evidence of changing or adapting their internal processes and working practices as a direct result of the co-creation endeavour. We believe that organisations would rarely accept to get involved in a co-creation process if they were not prepared to question their own organisational practices and beliefs. This implies that sales people need to:

1. Identify with whom and when to co-create
2. Develop relationships based on trust and transparency
3. Organise and manage multi-level dialogues

With whom and when to co-create

Co-creation requires a significant commitment and investment of resources from the organisations involved, particularly if organisational learning and innovation are to be generated. Thus, not every customer will be interested in entering into such a complex process, and some may prefer to focus on realising organisational efficiencies. In some industries there is an imperative to do more with less and with fewer people, which is a trend sales organisations need to acknowledge. This implies that sales people should only develop co-creation relationships with customers of strategic importance that are willing to engage in relationships of this nature.

Develop relationships based on trust and transparency

Developing co-creation focused relationships requires a constant dialogue. Close and deep interactions amongst the sales force, customers and partners are necessary. These dialogues are fuelled by high degrees of information shar-ing. Sharing valuable, often sensitive information in addition to high levels of involvement and process realignment increases complexity and risk in the relationship. Thus, a mind-set change is required to transform interactions and customer relationships from transactional to collaborative.

Organise and manage multi-level dialogues

In a co-creation approach, key organisational resources at the customer's and the supplier's side, must be redirected towards the co-creation process. For that reason interactions and dialogues are needed at multiple levels and across multiple functions within and between the organisations. These dialogues enable establishing multiple interactions, which lead to a climate of trust and transparency. The role of the sales person and her/his customer counterpart is to enable and to facilitate these contacts.

WHAT IS THE PROCESS OF CO-CREATION?

The co-creation model for sales people consists of inputs in the forms of capabilities, a process whereby the stakeholders i.e. the customers and the sales people complement each other's capabilities to build solutions, an outcome in the form of an experience and finally a degree of learning which feeds back into the capabilities of the organisation.

INPUT: CAPABILITIES

Capabilities typically refer to:
• Goods and services which are embedded into the existing value propositions of the organisation.
• Know-how, which are organisational capabilities such as designing an IT infrastructure, data analytics, managing events, software development etc.
• Partners, which are suppliers and third parties with specific capabilities of their own, which complement those of the organisation.
• Skills, which are the personal qualities of the people within the organisation.

PROCESS: CO-CREATION

Examples of co-creation activities include:
• Customer and partner selection, that is, the identification and prioritisation of the customers and partners with whom the supplier wants to co-create with.

• Information gathering, which is about understanding each other's jobs to be done and the capabilities each stakeholder can provide to help build the solution.
• Solution design, which is about conceptualising the solution that is needed to solve the customer's problem or realise the customer's opportunity. In this phase, agreements are also made about Intellectual Property Rights and other rights related to the commercialisation of the solution.
• Solution Development, which is about co-producing the solutions. This phase also includes the installation of the product/service and its use by the customer.

OUTCOME: EXPERIENCE

The ultimate aim of the co-creation approach is to create strong sustainable positive experiences. These experiences are often driven by emotional responses linked to changes in attitudes, preferences and mind-sets. Emotions and shifts in attitudes occur throughout the process whereby information will be exchanged, analysed and discussed generating alternatives to help achieve the customer's job to be done. During this process, customers interpret and assimilate information that contributes to the creation of their experiences. The customer behaves and makes decisions depending on their perceived role and their feelings during the process co-creation. In many ways, the behaviour will be the main driver behind the stakeholder's experience.

LEARNING: KNOW-HOW

Through co-creation, suppliers and customers can develop an increased capacity to learn how to deal with:

• Technology changes, by co-creating solutions based on new technologies, customers can discover how these technologies can help them to improve their business and suppliers can develop new capabilities implementing and servicing these new technologies.

• Market changes, transformations in regulations or demand can lead to radical new ways for suppliers to interact with their customers. By co-creating solutions to deal with specific market changes, customers can discover new ways to reach their customers or to develop new business models while suppliers can develop new capabilities about customer needs in specific industries and markets.

• Developing customer-supplier relationships, by engaging in a co-creation process to encourage people to challenge their current views and beliefs. Customers can discover new ways of doing things or new ways of looking at specific problems and for suppliers they can learn how their customers operate and how they can help them even more.

• Outsourcing none core activities, co-creation can help customers to identify areas where they would benefit from outsourcing to their suppliers: business processes that help optimise costs and to focus on their core activities. Suppliers can learn how to sell their value proposition as a managed service.

Perhaps the most important aspect is that the learning process that underpins co-creation enables the supplier to build new capabilities. This means that each time a supplier co-creates something with their customers they increase their own capabilities. If you take the premise that the value proposition is based on capabilities, this means that your organisation's offering can expand each time you co-create. This is different from selling, whereby the main benefit for the seller of selling products and services are the financial rewards. Each time you sell, you increase the financial but the organisation itself does not necessarily need to change or evolve. Co-creation also needs to be financially sustainable, however, the main difference with co-creation is that in addition to financial rewards, there are also opportunities for business transformation and offer development.

CAPABILITIES

PARTNERSHIP

LEARNING

72

BEKAERT CARDING SOLUTIONS

Bekaert is a global leader in the development and production of metallic wire-based materials used in manufacturing many different types of products globally. In the textile industry for instance, Bekaert manufactures special products used for carding fibres, such as balls of wool or cotton into individual strings. The process is achieved by passing wool or cotton through a set of cylinders covered with small spikes, which act like a come. This breaks up fibres and aligns them up into wires, which are then suitable for the weaving process. These spikes come in the form of wires, which are winded around the cylinders of the carding machine. Carding machines are considered very expensive thus need to be used at their maximum capacity. These machines are typically part of a production line, which only stops for maintenance purposes, such as replacing the spikes for the cylinders after they wore off. Bekaert sells the wire with the spikes and the service to wrap the wire and spikes on the cylinders. The actual cost of the wire and spikes is extremely low but is has large impact on the throughput and the quality of the output of the machine.

After purchasing a company, they discovered they had the license for the use of a university patent, a design for a new shape of spike applicable to carding processes. The new shape was unproven and was significantly more complex to manufacture. Bekaert decided that to further develop this patent into a commercial product they needed to collaborate with other manufacturers. These manufacturers had to be willing to take on the risk to test the new spikes on at least one of their production lines. To find a manufacturer who was willing to take the risk of using one of their production line to test a new product required the sales force to use a great deal of knowledge and persuasion. It also required a customer with whom a sales executive person had already developed a strong relationship and trust. After finding a customer and running some tests, they discovered that the throughput of the machine could be increased by 20%. In addition, the shape of the spikes creates less dust, reducing maintenance costs and helping realise substantial savings in material because of the fibres could be made thinner. In light of these results, Bekaert co-developed other geometric forms of the spikes for different types of end user applications.

PRINCIPLE 1:
FOCUS ON ENDS VERSUS MEANS

The objective here was clearly to co-develop a series of new spikes, which would affect the manufacturer's output. As one of the executives from Bekaert recognised, "Our sales people practically live at the customer in order to ensure the process runs fine".

PRINCIPLE 2:
TURN THE CUSTOMER INTO AN ACTIVE PARTNER

In this case, the customer was clearly a partner, as they were responsible for using their production line to test and evaluate the new spikes. The side effects such as, less dust and the need for less material to produce the same outputs, were discovered by the customer and not by Bekaert.

PRINCIPLE 3:
DEVELOP VALUE PROPOSITION BASED ON ORGANISATIONAL CAPABILITIES

Bekaert's capabilities comprised:
1. the newly designed spikes
2. the know how of how to further adjust the geometry of the spikes for various end user applications
3. the skills of the people involved in the development and the testing process
4. the license on the patent

The customer's capabilities comprised:
1. ability to test new spikes on their production lines
2. the know how of how to monitor and evaluate the results of the test
3. the skills of their people involved in the evaluation of the tests

PRINCIPLE 4:
FOCUS LEARNING THROUGH DIALOGUES AND BUILDING RELATIONSHIPS

The learning was triggered by the availability of a potential new technology and the drive to further optimise the manufacturing process. The customer learned about the impact of the spikes on their carding process and how it can be improved for various end user applications. Bekaert learned how different geometries affect the output process, which leads to the development of a new set of products. Import

in this case is that the co-creation was made possible based on the existing strong customer relationship. This relationship created the basis for dialogue and trust without which no co-creation and learning would have occurred. This case highlights an important question about the role of customer relationships in co-creation. Most cases we examined showed how co-creation enables further development of customer relationships. However close scrutiny also showed that prior to co-create, both supplier and customer already had some form of relationship. This is needed to create the level of trust for the customer and the supplier to embark in a co-creation process, which will require full transparency and sharing of information. So, how can you use co-creation as a means to attract new customers? At Bekaert, the ability to co-create in new product development is one of the elements, which are part of their value proposition. Most prospects would not start a relationship by co-creating immediately. They first want to setup a relationship with Bekaert but they know that once they have done that the opportunity to take the relationship further through co-creation is there.

This case also highlights an important question about where or how co-creation is initiated. The Bekaert case shows how co-creation came about triggered by an external event: suddenly realising they had a new patent. The strong relationships enabled them to take advantage of this event, but how can organisations promote or organise co-creation across their sales force? For that we need to design a service based on co-creation but which the sales people could propose pro-actively. So, let us now look at how we can develop a co-creation service.

CO-CREATION AS A SERVICE

For the customer to be willing to engage in a co-creation process with a supplier, superior value must be perceived over and above the (expected) value derived by the supplier's existing products and services. This perception can, in turn, be triggered by the customer experiencing problems that current available offerings are not addressing. The first task is to uncover which other problems your customers are still challenged with. Customer job mapping is a method, which allows doing just that. The second task involves building capabilities leveraging both the suppliers but also the customer's and other third parties' resources in order to address new, potentially complex problems.

CUSTOMER JOB MAPPING TOOLKIT

We need to understand the job the customer has to do and what their experience is doing that job. Based on this information we can start developing services that help the customer with these issues. In practice, understanding the needs of customers is something, which is difficult to assess. Simply asking the customer about their needs or using traditional research methods are proving to be unsuccessful when it comes to identify innovative ideas. Customers tend to have difficulty imagining services that they have not experienced yet. One way to uncover customer's latent needs is to focus on the outcomes, scenarios and mission the customer wishes to accomplish, in other words 'the job to be done'. As we already mentioned products and services, do not add value but instead they are used to create value for the customer. The customer does this by using the products and services to get specific jobs done.

According to Lance Bettencourt and Antony Ulwick , one way to uncover new ways to innovate is through job mapping[3]. Job mapping is the process by which the customer's "job-to-be-done" is broken down into discrete steps mapping out the complete journey. Most jobs can be broken down into "pre-work", "work" and "post-work". In the pre-work, the customer has to define what has to be done before the core execution steps. In the work-stage, the customer executes the core activities part of the job. In the post-work stage, the customer executes tasks that ensure the job delivers the desired outcomes. By investigating how customers experience each of these steps, suppliers can uncover new areas of customer dissatisfaction. It is however important to understand that the aim is not to map out the customer process as you would in a process improvement exercise. The main objective is to uncover areas where the customer is not reaching what they have set out to achieve and to identify the reasons why. It is important not to make any judgments about whether or not you could help the customer with their problems at this stage. The aim is to find areas with potential to co-create with the customer and not necessarily to solve the issue completely for them. As a supplier, you might be able to provide some capabilities, which in combination with the capabilities of your customer or with those of other organizations, the problem could be solved. In theory, once you have captured the customer's problems you could brainstorm about possible solutions. However, in our experience, the solution can often be envisaged (at least to a certain extent) by the customer, when the problem has been clearly diagnosed. The question is more about how you as a supplier can develop a service, which will help the customer to solve this problem.

Mapping the customer's job to be done typically consists of the following four dimensions:

1. Activities: What are the activities the customer performs during that stage?
2. Objectives: What is the customer trying to achieve during this stage?
3. Problems: What are the main problems, if any, the customer experiences during this stage? For each problem what are the main obstacles?
4. Opportunities: How could a supplier such as yourself help them with these problems?

These dimensions can be captured during an customer interview or afterwards to structure the input your received on the template below.

The template, on the following page, can be used to capture insights from a single customer or a single informant, or as a means to consolidate inputs received from several different customers.

	PRE WORK
ACTIVITIES	
CUSTOMER OBJECTIVES	
PROBLEMS	
POSSIBLE IMPROVEMENTS	

WORK	POST-WORK

TECHNOLOGY ROADMAP SERVICES

TNO is a Dutch research institute, with a focus on applied sciences. The organisation was established by law in 1932 by the Dutch government with the aim of strengthening innovation in industry and in government. Today TNO is an organisation of about 4.500 employees who provides innovation and specialist consultancy. It also grants licenses for patents and specialist software. The market sectors they are working on are; healthy living, industrial innovation, defence, safety and security, energy, transport and mobility, built environment and information society.

WHAT IS THE CUSTOMER'S JOB TO BE DONE?

Many of TNO's customers are high tech manufacturing organisations whose job consists of constantly being on the lookout for trends in the market. These trends are important in order to inform their product development roadmaps, which often look 10 to even 20 years into the future. Scenario planning and other business planning methods are all used to ensure that the product roadmap is aligned with key evolutions in the market. The main problem is to accurately predict market and technology trends while looking so many years in advance. This creates uncertainty, which is exacerbated if in the past such

predictions turned out to be wrong. The second problem when developing such roadmaps is to accurately define the sequence in which the markets will evolve. It may also require a consortium of technology, government and research organisations to collaborate. This requires an alignment of all parties in terms of their vision of the future.

WHAT IS THE SOLUTION AND HOW IS IT CO-CREATED WITH THE CUSTOMER?

TNO offers their customers the opportunity to benchmark their technology roadmap with the one TNO has or to develop a roadmap together from scratch. Developing various technology roadmaps looking several years in the future is one of TNO's core activities in order to help the government's purpose to build and promote innovation within the Dutch industry. Being an independent non-profit organisation makes TNO an ideal partner for many organisations and research institutions to collaborate with. As a result, TNO has access to a vast network of technology experts both in the industry and in the scientific research community. All of these experts can be called upon to help develop a roadmap with a customer.

PRINCIPLE 1:
FOCUS ON ENDS VERSUS MEANS

TNO's main non-governmental revenues come from commissioned research or joint licensing programs of specific technologies they co-developed. However, in order for the industry to commission TNO with such work they all need a clearly defined technology roadmap. Developing such technology roadmaps are not an end itself but rather a means for TNO to get commission research work later. The whole process relies on the ability to share knowledge and insight among partners, which can be TNO and one customer or a whole consortium of organisations.

PRINCIPLE 2:
TURN THE CUSTOMER INTO AN ACTIVE PARTNER

Whether the exercise consists of developing a joint roadmap from scratch or to benchmark an existing roadmap, the customer has to get involved in the exercise. Without their active involvement in the process, TNO cannot build or benchmark their roadmap. When several organisations are involved, the results get even more powerful due to the combined intelligence.

PRINCIPLE 3:
DEVELOP VALUE PROPOSITIONS BASED ON ORGANISATIONAL CAPABILITIES

TNO's value proposition, consist of three main capabilities. The first is TNO's own expertise in particular technologies. For the customer this means having access to people with real in-depth expertise in their domain. The second is TNO's network of industrial, governmental and research institutions, which can be brought in to establish collaboration on the roadmap exercise when and if needed. The last capability is TNO's own roadmap methodology that allows developing a technology roadmap and aligning multiple stakeholders.

PRINCIPLE 4:
FOCUS ON LEARNING THROUGH DIALOGUES AND BUILDING RELATIONSHIPS

The customer learns about which developments they need to schedule in the future and how to prioritise them. TNO learns about the future technology developments, which enable them to initiate technology research projects with governments, universities and industries.

	PRE WORK
ACTIVITIES	Analyse Market and Technology Trends Analyse own Strengths and Weaknesses Develop a product strategy.
CUSTOMER OBJECTIVES	Define the product strategy for the coming X years.
PROBLEMS	Feeling of uncertainty about strategy due to the high amount inter-dependencies with other technologies.
POSSIBLE IMPROVEMENTS	We want the ability to cross-check our product roadmaps with other technology manufacturers and researchers.

WORK	POST-WORK
Translate the future vision and strategy into workable product development roadmap	Evaluate constantly the assumptions upon which the roadmap is made and adapt the roadmap where needed.
Develop a product roadmap	Keeping the product roadmap up to date.
Feeling of uncertainty about the correct sequence of the all the technology evolutions.	Changes might not be spotted in the market.
We want some feedback and input from researchers and other manufacturers in our industry on how to implement our strategy.	We need more eyes to scan the market and technology evolutions in order to make sure we spot changes on time.

BUSINESS BANKING

WHAT IS THE CUSTOMER'S JOB TO BE DONE?

A business bank identified among their clients in the small to medium enterprise segment a need for business advice regarding particular strategic decisions. Because these organisations are small, they often do not have the financial resources to pay for the services of business consulting organisations. Yet, they do need and seek advice to increase their confidence about the strategic decisions they are going to make.

WHAT IS THE SOLUTION AND HOW IS IT CO-CREATED WITH THE CUSTOMER?

While many executives seek advice, they also found that many other successful entrepreneurs were willing to provide advice and share their experience. By connecting both the manager who seeks advice with the professional who has the experience and who is willing to share it the bank is effectively enabling and helping its customers' strategy making and decision making processes. For an account manager from the bank, this is not very different from the role they already have. They currently bring in the right product expert to the customer depending on the type of financing they need. Now they also brokering relationships and bringing together business experts depending on the type of business problem the customer has (irrespective of whether the nature of the problem is financial or not). The difference here is that the bank will call upon the capabilities of its own customers to supply that service.

PRINCIPLE 1: FOCUS ON ENDS VERSUS MEANS

The objective is to help the customer to make the best possible strategic decision, which may or may not lead to the need for a financial service. From an account planning perspective, the account manager is concerned with the business decision the customer is making and how they can help their customer in making these decisions. From a risk management perspective, all account managers in the banking industry follow up their customers after they provided the funds to insure they will be repaid. In this case the account manager does not only monitor the customer, he or she can also help them by putting them in contact with other customers to help them turning their investment into a financial success.

PRINCIPLE 2:
TURN THE CUSTOMER INTO AN ACTIVE PARTNER

The customers are becoming partners of the bank by offering their advice to others. The bank also becomes the partner of their customer by helping them to make the best possible business decision.

PRINCIPLE 3:
DEVELOP VALUE PROPOSITIONS BASED ON ORGANISATIONAL CAPABILITIES

The bank clearly positions itself in a role of partner looking for areas where their customers need help. Their capabilities are the knowledge and capabilities of the bank and of their customers. This service enables the account manager to change the dialogue from interest rates towards offering advice and business support to their customers.

PRINCIPLE 4:
FOCUS ON LEARNING THROUGH DIALOGUES AND BUILDING RELATIONSHIPS

The main challenge for the bank is to maintain the dialogue going between them and their customers. The main area of learning for the bank is on building communities and managing dialogues between them and their customers.

	PRE WORK
ACTIVITIES	Analyse market trends. Analyse own strengths and weaknesses. Develop a business strategy.
CUSTOMER OBJECTIVES	Define the business strategy and objectives.
PROBLEMS	Feeling of uncertainty about our strategy especially when it involves large investments.
POSSIBLE IMPROVEMENTS	We want some feedback and input to formulate our strategy.

WORK	POST-WORK
Look for financing solutions. Make the needed investments. Implement the changes.	Assess the return on the investments made. Adapt the strategy where needed and implement changes.
Implement the strategy.	Keeping the strategy up to date.
Feeling of uncertainty about our strategy especially when it involves large investments.	The large investments have been made they better work.
We want some feedback and input about how to implement our strategy.	We want some feedback and input about how to get the most out of our strategy.

CO-CREATION AND THE CUSTOMER BUYING PROCESS

In the previous chapter, we introduced the different stages of a typical buying process for B2B customers. We concluded that, in the future, sales people will have to add value either by helping their customers making their strategic plans or by helping them to increase the efficiency and effectiveness of their operations when using the supplier's products. Many of the examples tend to focus on helping the customer to develop their strategy. So, let us look at an example of Michelin helps their customers to make the most out of their tyres.

CO-CREATION AND KEY ACCOUNT MANAGEMENT

The need for ongoing dialogue, trust and relationships leads us to believe that key account management and co-creation share a number of dimensions and elements. In our view, this is not the case. We now describe a case of account management in a business bank, which illustrate a number of account management processes used in sales organisations across industries, so differences between account management and co-creation can be established.

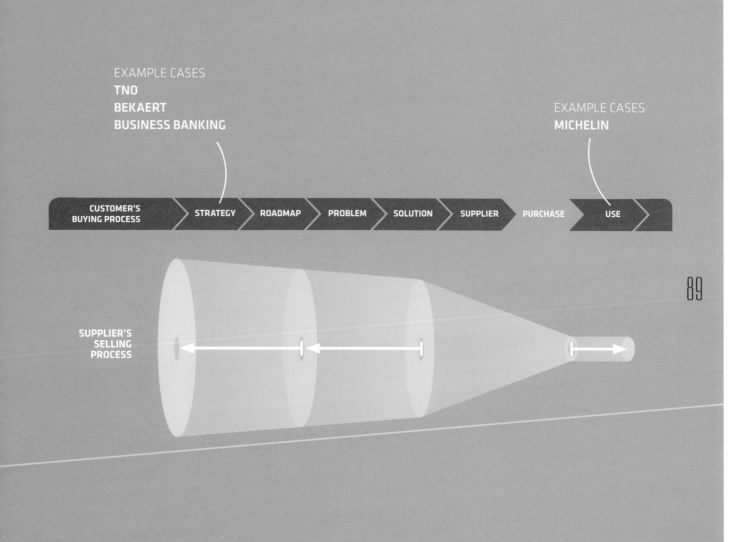

EXAMPLE CASES
TNO
BEKAERT
BUSINESS BANKING

EXAMPLE CASES
MICHELIN

CUSTOMER'S BUYING PROCESS > **STRATEGY** > **ROADMAP** > **PROBLEM** > **SOLUTION** > **SUPPLIER** > PURCHASE > **USE** >

SUPPLIER'S SELLING PROCESS

89

MICHELIN FLEET SOLUTION[4]

WHAT IS THE CUSTOMER'S JOB TO BE DONE?

Michelin noticed that in a key market, the road transportation industry, many of their customers where consolidating due to globalisation. The market was beginning to be dominated by fewer but much larger transportation companies who tend to regard tyres as a pure commodity constantly shopping around for the best possible deal. Despite being a commodity, tyres do have a great impact on the efficiency of the transport. Tyre related breakdowns do cause major delays and costs to the journeys. In addition, the condition of the tyres has an impact on the fuel consumption of vehicles. These are considerations, which need to be taken into account when purchasing new tyres but also when maintaining them. One of the main 'jobs to be done' is to ensure that the tyres are well serviceable while minimising the amount of time a truck is not on the road. In order to address these issues transport companies need to find ways to optimise their tyre sourcing and management activities.

WHAT IS THE SOLUTION AND HOW IS IT CO-CREATED WITH THE CUSTOMER?

Since managing tyres is not a core activity for any large transportation company, Michelin proposed its customers to outsource tyre-related activities to them. This means that for a monthly fee Michelin would not only supply the tyres but also maintain and repair them. Such a service requires a vast geographical presence, which is needed to provide the required maintenance and repair work. This is achieved by converting Michelin's distribution network into a service network, which will perform the maintenance and repairs on their behalf. For this solution to work three parties must collaborate, the customer, the distributor and Michelin, the manufacturer.

The Fleet Solution Offer provides customers with: peace of mind, better cost control (lower fuel costs, less breakdowns, better operational management, less administrative burden) and the benefits from Michelin continuous innovations. For the distributor networking the solution ensures them that Michelin will bring them business, it will enable them to widen the scope of their own services and capabilities and lastly it will enable them to service large international transportation companies which normally would not do business with them. For Michelin the solution enables them to avoid being seen as a commodity supplier and to develop deep, long lasting customer relationships.

PRINCIPLE 1:
FOCUS ON ENDS VERSUS MEANS

The solution is no longer about selling tyres to customers but about delivering them the value of using Michelin tyres. This implies a new business model for Michelin whereby managing the customer's tyres is becoming one of their core activities. This also changes the relationship between Michelin and their distributors. They are no longer just a channel selling tyres into different markets but they are an essential part of Michelin's value proposition. They will have to ensure the quality standards of Michelin and in return, Michelin will bring them new business.

PRINCIPLE 2:
TURN THE CUSTOMER INTO A PARTNER

The role of the customer in this solution does not really change. This means that the solution is no really developed with them but sold to them. The selling itself has become much more complex. The partnership element in this solution is mainly between Michelin and the distributors who have to co-create the service and the ultimate customer experience closely together.

PRINCIPLE 3:
DEVELOP VALUE PROPOSITIONS BASED ON ORGANISATIONAL CAPABILITIES

The sales process between Michelin and the customer has completely changed. The dialogue is no longer about tyres, so product knowledge is of very limited use to the sales force. The sales process is about selling value and making sure the customer understands and sees it. The value proposition relies on the ability of Michelin to operate such a service and on the quality of their distribution network. The ability to understand the customer's business is essential for the sales person in order to calculate the right pricing. The tyre itself has become a vehicle to deliver the actual service to the customer but it is no longer the value proposition.

PRINCIPLE 4:
FOCUS ON LEARNING THROUGH DIALOGUES AND RELATIONSHIPS

With each new customer, Michelin increases their ability to manage their distribution network in order to deliver the right service at the right price. By engaging in deep customer relationships the sales people learn about the customer and are better equipped to adopt better pricing strategies in order to keep the relationship profitable. These learning are essential as incorrect assessments of the customer's business leads to an unprofitable relationship.

	PRE WORK
ACTIVITIES	Define tyre requirements, compare products, negotiate and purchase.
CUSTOMER OBJECTIVES	Get the best prices possible for the tyres which in our view is a commodity.
PROBLEMS	How can we centralize all tyre purchases and other tyre related processes across our business?
POSSIBLE IMPROVEMENTS	We want a solution to centralise our tyre purchasing and management activities across all business units.

WORK	POST-WORK
Use, maintain and repair the tyres.	Evaluate tyre effectiveness overall. Dispose of old tyres.
The Least possible hassle with the tyres.	See how we can improve the efficiency of our trucks.
How can we reduce the number of tyre related breakdowns?, How can combine tyre maintenance and keeping the trucks driving on the road?	How could we reduce fuel consumptions through better or different tyres? How can we reduce our carbon footprint?
We want to keep our trucks driving while making our tyres last as long as possible.	We want to keep out trucks driving while making our tyres last as long as possible.

ACCOUNT MANAGEMENT PROCESS

In this example, we look at the key account planning process of a large international business bank. Each account manager has a portfolio of about 50 accounts to manage. In the period between November and December, they visit most of their customers to learn about their business plans for the coming year. Based on this information the account manager completes her/his account plans. The process mainly consists of identifying which new investment the customer will make in the coming year. Depending upon the type of investments, they identify which products and services they will propose for their customer. This next step consists of forecasting their revenues for their customer in the coming year. Based on the forecast, they schedule a number of customer visits for them and their various product specialists.

WHAT IS THE CUSTOMER'S JOB TO BE DONE?

From the customer's perspective, the job to be done is to decide whether or not to do the investment and ensure they get the funding from the bank for it. In that respect the visit from the account manager to learn about the customer's plans may be useful for them to learn about possible issues they may face obtaining the financing. The customer makes many other issues running the organisation but helping the customer to solve them is not part of the account manager's role.

IS THIS CO-CREATION?

PRINCIPLE 1: FOCUS ON ENDS VERSUS MEANS

The purpose of the account plan is for the account manager to make a forecast of products and services to be sold. The bank does position itself as a partner who helps their customer to achieve their business objectives. However, the partnership is limited to selling their customer their financial services when the customer needs it. The bank is obviously concerned about whether the customer achieves their business objectives. On the one side, because they want to make sure they get their money back but also because it provides the bank with further business opportunities. However, the bank itself does not do anything to help the customer to achieve their business objectives. That is entirely up to the customer.

PRINCIPLE 2: TURN THE CUSTOMER INTO AN ACTIVE PARTNER

The focus is on matching standard products and services, which may be combined to form some kind of solution for the customer. The focus is nevertheless on product and services.

94

PRINCIPLE 3:
DEVELOP VALUE PROPOSITIONS BASED ON ORGANISATIONAL CAPABILITIES

The aim of their account management approach is to build close relationships with their customers in order to keep them satisfied and loyal. In these relationships, both the customers and the account managers have discrete roles.

PRINCIPLE 4:
FOCUS ON LEARNING THROUGH DIALOGUES AND BUILDING RELATIONSHIPS

The making of the account plan is based on one or two visits whereby the customer informed the account manager about their business plans for the upcoming period. Further visits with the customer will be planned based on the individual business opportunities identified by the account manager. In this case, the account manager learns about the customer's intentions and the customer learns about potential issues about their upcoming financing needs.

This case is clearly not a case of co-creation. To transform this into a co-creation process would require substantial more resources and time to be spent on the customer. In this case, the bank would not want to do that. Let us now imagine the customer would be worth investing more time and effort into. How would that affect the process? In most cases, we observed the result is that the account managers tend to spend more time analysing the customer's writing the account plan in more detail. The process however, does not really change. Customers, even the strategic ones, often remain in their role of informants and little is done to co-create an account plan with the customer. So, how could you change this process and turn it into a co-creation one? First, we will have to change the initial visit into a two-way dialogue whereby the customer will not be an informant but an active participant. Second, the resulting plan will have to be shared and validated by both the customer and the supplier. During our interviews we came across one, IT consulting organisation that was willing to share how they make their account plans with their strategic customers.

CO-CREATING AN ACCOUNT PLAN

This organisation has about 20 strategic accounts, which are managed by a few key account directors. These account directors act as account managers but have a director's role within the organisation, which give them the authority to mandate resources needed to manage their accounts.

WHAT IS THE CUSTOMER'S JOB TO BE DONE?

The customer's job to be done consists of defining and implementing the IT strategy which is most likely to achieve the objectives the IT managers received from their management. To implement their projects these IT managers rely on a variety of suppliers to supply expertise and equipment to these projects. Their main problem is to find the right suppliers and partner with whom they can develop strong relationships allowing them to ensure their projects will run on time and on budget. Beside that they also require suppliers who can help them to translate their objectives into concrete solutions and projects to be implemented.

HOW IS THE SOLUTION CO-CREATED WITH THE CUSTOMER?

The account planning process is with a two-day workshop. The participants include all the consultants who are working on the customer's projects and the key team members from the customer's side. The workshop is focussed on the customer's main IT and business challenges. Through this process, the consultants learn about the customer's customers, which are the business users, and what their needs and challenges are. The participants are asked on several occasions to brainstorm about how they believe these problems could be addressed drawing on their vast experience working on projects at different customers. By helping the customer to find solutions to address their IT challenges, the consultants position themselves as partners. The consultants will also share their strategy and business objectives to the customer, during the workshop. The aim is to show the customer what type of capabilities they are developing internally; with the aim to identify projects, which they might start with the customer allowing them to further develop these capabilities.

What follows is a set of recommendations to improve current working relationships and new ideas for future business opportunities, which are added to the overall key account plan. The outcome is an account plan, which is for a large part created in collaboration between the customer and the supplier. The plan is formally validated by the customer and by all the internal stakeholders before being presented and accepted internally.

PRINCIPLE 1
FOCUS ON ENDS VERSUS MEANS

The account management processes are focused on helping the IT department addressing their challenges. The IT consultants position themselves clearly as partners focussing on helping their customer rather than selling additional resources.

PRINCIPLE 2
TURN THE CUSTOMER INTO AN ACTIVE PARTNER

The outcome of the whole process is an account plan in which all the future opportunities for collaboration are identified, quantified and validated by all parties. This means that a large part of the sales process has already been completed. The only thing left now are the final negotiations when the individual projects are started. The fact that the consultants are willing to share openly with the customer what business opportunities they see demonstrate the amount of trust and partnership that exists. This level of trust is needed in order co-create the account plan together.

PRINCIPLE 3
DEVELOP VALUE PROPOSITIONS BASED ON ORGANISATIONAL CAPABILITIES

The aim of the account planning process is to identify the customer's challenges and to find ways in which the consultants can collaborate to address them. To implement these solutions both the customer and the consultants will call upon their ecosystem of partners and suppliers to supply the needed capabilities.

PRINCIPLE 4
FOCUS ON LEARNING THROUGH DIALOGUES AND BUILDING RELATIONSHIPS

The way in which the consultants and their customer collaborate is clearly based on on-going dialogues, which happens at multiple levels of both organisations. The aim of this case is to provide some source of inspiration about changing a one-sided activity, such as account planning, into a co-created one.

	PRE WORK
ACTIVITIES	Identify possible to solutions to achieve our IT objectives. Translate the solutions into a project roadma
CUSTOMER OBJECTIVES	Define our IT strategy to achieve objectives.
PROBLEMS	Uncertainty about how to implement the IT strategy.
POSSIBLE IMPROVEMENTS	We want partners who is able to help us.

WORK	POST-WORK
Implement IT projects.	Change management. Project evaluations. Adapt project roadmaps and solutions.
Projects are implemented on time and on budget.	Deliver solutions that the user community want to use. Identify and remedy projects which are running behind on time and budget.
Finding partners or suppliers which can help us to achieve our objectives.	
We want a partner who is committed to help us completing our projects on time and on budget.	

HOW TO DESIGN A CO-CREATION SERVICE?

Many organisations we interviewed reported examples of co-creation but also mentioned that only a few people in their organisation were actually capable or motivated to do it. All the other sales people lacked the knowledge and/or experience to actually carry on this approach with their customers. Fearful of the unknown and uncontrollable, and thus, the possibility of damaging the relationship with their customers, most sales people do not dare to introduce such an approach in their selling methods if they are not familiar with it. What some sales people lack is a well-designed, validated method that can be replicated for co-creation. The co-creation approach can often replace traditional sales processes. In effect, the sales process becomes a service process delivering value to the customer. This is an essential step in order to move towards a stage where the customer will pay to participate in such a service.

Co-Creation is a process, and if an organisation wants to systematise this into a method used by the whole of the sales force it needs to be designed into a service. Service blueprinting is a method to graphically develop and visualise service processes. In each step of the process, the actions and the contact point of the customer with the organisation becomes visible. It is very similar to process mapping. The main difference is that with service blue printing the customer interactions are central to the design. Focussing on the differences between the customer's activities and the one from the supplier is an essential part of service blue printing. It is a process map with a strong emphasis on the customer perspective. The aim is to see the service from the customer's perspective and from the supplier perspective. This makes it so relevant in a co-creation process. Like with engineers or architects blueprints are used to communicate the process with customers, partners and colleagues. The overall blueprint contains a visual representation of all the interactions between all the stakeholders of the service. This allows all the stakeholders to understand their respective roles in the co-creation process with the customer. A service blueprint process contains usually the following five components: Customers activities, Evidence, visible employee activities (called on stage), invisible employee activities (called backstage) and support processes. All the activities, which are on stage, are visible to the customer and above the line of visibility. Underneath the line are all the backstage activities, which the customer does not see.

Let us look at one more example from the IT industry and see how they designed their co-creation service.

Service Blueprint

Service Name ....

Date...

ONSTAGE

EVIDENCE

CUSTOMER ACTION

line of interaction

FRONT LINE

line of visibility

BACKSTAGE

BACK OFFICE EMPLOYEES

line of internal interaction

SUPPORT PROCESSES

CGI'S SPARK INNOVATION CENTRE

WHAT IS THE CUSTOMER'S JOB TO BE DONE?

CGI, formally known as Logica, noticed that many of their customers invested over the past decade in many different IT technologies. Most customers invested in these new technologies scared to lose out on some new technologies. Today, having invested in so many new technologies some of which do not always deliver to the promised benefits, IT managers are becoming more careful in deciding what to invest in. They are also very wary about suppliers trying to convince them about new technologies based on slideshow presentations. Nevertheless, they still need to stay informed about new technologies and how they can improve their business. According to CGI, customers like to experience, first-hand, new technologies to assess its potential. They also want proof that the suppliers know the technology.

HOW IS THE SOLUTION CO-CREATED WITH THE CUSTOMER?

As a response, CGI developed a set of SPARK centres in their offices around the world. Each SPARK centre is managed by a team, which manages an innovation strategy comprising short (<1y), medium (<2y) and long-term (<3y) innovation. The SPARK centre only demonstrates short-term innovations for which demo prototype applications already exist. Medium and long-term innovations are projects, which are worked on in collaboration with other business partners and academic institutions. Each centre across the world has a set of themes on which they are the specialists and for which they have thought leaders. These thought leaders are typically consultants with a specific role and who are evaluated not based on billable days but based on the number of presentations, white papers written, and other activities directly related to the promotion of the innovation centre.

Allowing customers to see, touch and feel new technologies in the SPARK centre already creates a positive experience. Allowing them to participate in finding and implementing new innovative applications allow them to be involved in the process itself. Through these emotions and activities, the customers can learn about how new technologies can help them to improve their business.

PRINCIPLE 1:
FOCUS ON ENDS VERSUS MEANS

The means is the technology and the end is the impact this technology has on the customer's business. The aim of CGI is not about selling technology but about finding new possible applications for the technology and evaluating their impact on the customer's business. The proof of concept enables them to test and learn in the customer's organisation. Based on the learning the customer decides whether to invest in the new application or not. The end is to ensure that the customer gets the most out of their proof of concept.

PRINCIPLE 2:
TURN THE CUSTOMER INTO AN ACTIVE PARTNER

Because these new technologies are often unproven CGI first test the technology in their labs known as SPARK centres. The SPARK centres are used as the platform to test and brainstorm with their customers about potential uses for new emerging technologies. Out of this process comes a proof of concept. The outcome for the customer is the ability to be involved and co-create new potential applications for emerging technologies. Even if the brainstorm does not result in a proof of concept, they learn about the new technologies that are emerging and how they may affect their business. Because they can see, touch and feel these new technologies in the SPARK centres and later in their own organisation, creates an emotional feeling of excitement, which is key for this sort of innovative projects.

PRINCIPLE 3:
DEVELOP VALUE PROPOSITIONS BASED ON ORGANISATIONAL CAPABILITIES

Technology organisations such as CGI developed a competency, which is that of anticipating new technologies that are making it to the market. This competency enables them co-create a vision of how technologies can help their clients in the near future.

PRINCIPLE 4:
LEARNING THROUGH DIALOGUES AND RELATIONSHIPS

The SPARK centre enables CGI to start a dialogue about IT innovation with their customers.
CGI needs to establish its credibility and reputation as strategic IT partner. For that reason the centres are currently managed as cost centres. For the sales people it enables them to position themselves as a highly innovative organisation in the eyes of their customers. It enables them to learn more about their customer and how they see their business in the future. It also enables them to develop new business opportunities, which based on slideshows and brochures may not have happened.

	PRE WORK
ACTIVITIES	Meeting with IT suppliers. Attend seminars. Read magazines.
CUSTOMER OBJECTIVES	Finding new interesting technologies.
PROBLEMS	Too many slideshows.
POSSIBLE IMPROVEMENTS	We want to see, touch and feel the technology before making a decision.

WORK	POST-WORK
Implement the new technology for a small project.	Use and maintain the technology and solution.
Helping our business users to find ways to be more competitive through IT technology.	Helping our business users to get the most out of the solution.
We do not want to be the testing ground for our IT suppliers.	We have many new technologies that do not deliver any real added value.
Finding the right IT partner who has already some experience with the new technology.	Finding the right IT partner who is able to help us to define the added value before we implement the technology.

HOW IS THE SERVICE OFFERED?

These SPARK centres are a platform to promote and inspire customers about new technologies and how they could affect their business. Through these SPARK centres CGI demonstrates their capabilities regarding new IT technologies. The co-creation process consists of the following activities:

STEP 1 A thought leader (specialist consultant) identifies a business possibility at a customer

STEP 2 The thought leader invites the customer for a session at the spark centre.

STEP 3 The meeting is prepared among spark centre managers and thought leaders.

STEP 4 A demo of new technologies and possible applications regarding a specific topic is presented to the customers.

STEP 5 A brainstorm session with the customer is held on how the technology they have seen could be useful to their business.

STEP 6 The ideas, which emerged from the brainstorm, are further refined in a workable proof of concept proposal by the thought leaders.

STEP 7 The customer attends a second workshop session to further define the scope and the project plan for a proof of concept.

STEP 8 The proof of concept is implemented with the customer.

STEP 9 The customer evaluates outcomes of the proof of concept and decides whether to roll it out as a project.

Service Blueprint

ONSTAGE	EVIDENCE	
	CUSTOMER ACTION	Meeting with sales person
	line of **interaction**	
	FRONT LINE	Sales Visit Inv
	line of **visibility**	
BACKSTAGE	BACK OFFICE EMPLOYEES	Prepa
	line of **internal interaction**	
	SUPPORT PROCESSES	

Service Name ....

Date..

	In the SPARK centre		Proposal for a POC	at the customer		Project Proposal
efine ives sion.	Attends the workshops	Participate in the workshop	Accepts / Reject Proposal of POC	Collaborate implementing the POC	Evaluate POC	Budgets and Plans the Project
and align es	Present new technologies and facilitate the brainstorm		Develop a POC proposal	implementing the POC		Develop Project Proposal
ner visit	Book and setup the SPARK centre		Develop POC, Planning and Pricing for proposal	Resource Scheduling		Develop project, Planning and Pricing for proposal
	Prepare the room and catering		Resource Planning			Resource Planning

SUMMARY

All of the examples in this chapter are cases where the customer actually wants to co-create and get involved in the process. These are not 'sales tricks' that help sales people to persuade their customers to act in a pre-defined way. The customers who decide to participate know very well what the benefits are for the sales person but they also see the benefits they can derive from the co-creation process for them and for their organisations. This works when the customer trusts the sales person and their organisation but also when they can clearly see how the process works. The customer sees that is not a sales trick learned during a two-day sales training course and aimed at persuading the customer to give them more business. If there is one thing we learned out in our research, is that becoming a consultant and co-creating with your customer requires new organisational capabilities, it is an organisational phenomena not an individual one. This is not something that can be simply trained; this is something that requires organisational transformation and mindset change.

Moreover, not all your customers will want to co-create with you and even if they do they will not want to do that all the time. Their perception of value depends strongly on the situation they are in. Depending on their situation, they may want to co-create or they want to shop for the best price. The main difficulty here is that sales people need to learn how to qualify quickly which approach the customer is willing to follow. Doing this right depends here as well on a good understanding of the customer's job to be done. By analysing where the customer is in their internal process, you can determine which approach has the most value for them. The other difficulty is for the sales people to master several sales approaches proficiently. This is how the matrix sales organisations, which combine both product/technical sales people and account manager, may have a real advantage. Depending on the situation of the customer, the right sales person takes the lead.

Chapter 4

FROM CUSTOMER TO ASSET MANAGEMENT

WHAT ARE CUSTOMER-BASED ASSETS?

Sales, and more particularly account management, is undergoing a paradigm shift in many organisations. This shift involves a change in focus from managing customer accounts based on revenues to managing the accounts based on profitability. This change has been triggered by many organisations realising that the number of their customers has declined while the size of their large customers has increased. This is often the result of an ever-rising globalised business-to-business environment whereby a very large proportion of a suppliers' overall revenue stream is generated by a very small number of customers. To achieve their objectives, organisations depend on fewer, but much larger customers. These large customers are often the result of a close relationship that has been built over a period of many years. Large customers often become strategic customers as well given their influential role in offering development and innovation. Some businesses find that the total number of new customers they could acquire during a period of time like a year cannot compensate losing such a customer. Strategic customers are decisive in reaching the organisation's sales targets. Many sales organisations responded to this situation by implementing key account management teams and procedures within their organisations whereby each individual strategic customer is considered as a valuable asset for the company[1]. These intangible assets are critical and often important drivers of an organisation's value. The professionals managing these strategic customers are no longer in a purely sales role, but in one that can be described as business managers. Their task is to closely follow up and develop the web of relationships and interactions with the key customer, and to implement key account plans that will deliver mutual sustainable business growth. The nature of the relationships and investments the organisation is willing to make for these customers are characterized by commitment to the long-term.

A LOYAL CUSTOMER DOES NOT MEAN A PROFITABLE CUSTOMER

While the link between customer satisfaction and profitability is one of the cornerstones

Acquiring a new customer is more expensive that to retain an existing customer.

of customer relationship management which gained wide acceptance in the 1990's, more recent research found that the relationship between loyalty and profitability is weaker and more subtle than the proponents of loyalty programmes claim. In their research professors Reinartz (INSEAD) and Kumar (Georgia State University) found little or no evidence to suggest that customers in a business-to-business environment who purchase steadily from a supplier over time are necessarily cheaper to serve, less price sensitive, or particularly effective at bringing in new business[2] . Very large customers are powerful and often demand highly customised solutions, have high expectations in terms of sales and account management investments, and are challenging in terms of profit given their ability to negotiate better price terms. Large customers with professionalised procurement functions know their value to their suppliers and use it to obtain premium services or price discounts[3]. They are also typically more knowledgeable about product and service offerings (they have other points of comparison) and are better able to assess the quality and capabilities of a supplier. Purchasing has become a more strategic function in many businesses with huge impact on profitability, cost control and as a result, shareholder's value. Furthermore, many organisations recognise the strategic value-adding potential of global procurement and have, therefore, adopted integrated centralised purchasing processes and structures, furthering their bargaining power[4]. These are some of the reasons why customer profitability needs to be measured and managed carefully. Many organisations discover after conducting a detailed analysis of the profitability of their customers, that some of their large customers are in fact unprofitable customers[5]. Since the ultimate objective of companies is to make a profit from selling products and services, measuring and managing customer profitability has become an essential part of customer relationship management. Performance targets such as sales revenues and market

Customer satisfaction leads to customer loyalty and to ultimately customer profitability.

share growth ignore the impact of sales decisions on elements such as inventory, working capital needs, cost of capital, and their effect on the long-term relationship with the customer. The responsibility for managing these elements is not limited to accounting or logistics. They are also the responsibility of the sales professionals. Increasingly, sales people are made responsible, not only to manage their customer revenues but also their total profitability, in particular of the most strategic customers. In other words, sales people managing these accounts need up-to-date and detailed account profitability figures in order to determine the right prices and agree on the right service levels to ensure relevant costs to serve. One example of the emphasis on profitability is provided by a large European telecommunications operator that defined a rate of return for each type of their customers. Sales people have the freedom to allocate discounts or offer extra services as they see fit as long as the return of the overall accounts remains within the set rates. This requires almost sophisticated and regular reporting of each customer's profitability level.
As the nature of selling to large accounts is changing towards co-creating solutions with customers and partners, detailed cost accounting at a customer level is an absolute requirement in order to ensure that the overall business remains profitable.

MARKET BASED ASSETS

Think about the value of companies such as Facebook, Amazon, Yahoo or Google. Their value is not determined by current profitability but instead it is based on their future potential. This is the difference between book value and market value, whereby the market value is often a multiple of the book value. So, why would someone value a company at more than what it is valued on paper? The reason is that the book value does not include the market-based assets of a company such as customers. At the time of writing this book, the market value of Facebook is almost six times more than its book value. Google's market value is eleven times and Amazon's market value is fifteen times more than their book value. While there are several sources of market-based assets for many organisations, their customers are the largest one. Traditionally it has been very difficult to define and measure the market value of customers other than the book value of the deals they close. However, there is growing recognition that a significant proportion of the organisation's value lies in market assets, which are off balance sheet assets. With the consolidation in many sectors it means that there are fewer, but much bigger, customers. Getting on their supplier list and establishing long-term relationships with them creates value for the organisation. Leveraging such assets requires organisations to look beyond the traditional input and output of sales analysis. Businesses need to look at the consequences of sales decisions on the organisation's cash flows in the longer term. Similarly, decisions on how to manage a customer cannot rely only on the current profitability of a customer but also needs to take into account the customer's future potential.

How much importance does your organisation places on current profitability to determine your key customers?

CALCULATING FUTURE ORIENTED CUSTOMER PROFITABILITY

In our research, we have found that many sales organisations place much more importance on the current profitability of their customers than on the future potential. This seems reasonable since current profitability is a fact while future potential is an estimation and therefore more difficult to ascertain. Moreover, the sales costs to attract and retain customers are booked as expenses and are not depreciated over time, thus customer value is a concept not widely implemented in organizations. Anecdotal evidence from our workshops and seminars shows how when account mangers define customer attractiveness criteria current sales revenues are rated very highly while revenue potential is not widely considered. This would mean that prospect customers will rarely be attractive. The reality in many organizations is somehow different. When estimating the customer value in a business-to-business environment the past may not be an adequate predictor for the future. Future-oriented customer profitability, calculates the net present value of future expected costs and revenues associated with serving a customer over its lifetime, thus known as customer lifetime value (CLV). This approach to calculate customer profitability is useful to:

1. Rank Order your customers. By using CLV an organisation can rank order its customers or classify them into tiers based on their expected profitability. This allows organisations to appropriately allocate resources across the customer portfolio.

2. Define acquisition strategy. CLV can also be used for making customer acquisition decisions such that an organisation does not spend more on acquiring a customer than the CLV of that customer. It allows organisations to balance their resources between customer acquisition and customer retention.

3. Define the value of the organisation. Recent studies also show that CLV can provide a link between customer value and the organisation's value. The CLVs of all the current and potential customers form a firm's customer equity, which is sometime used as a proxy to measure the firm's equity-market. Thus, the CLV framework helps align marketing and finance metrics.

Does this mean that we should no longer set targets based on short-term profitability? Not necessarily. What we are suggesting is that organisations set targets on short- term sales but also on long-term value creation. We have found several organisations that focus on long-term value creation and define measures and targets that are consistent with this focus. Performance targets in general should be consistent with measures of customer value so to foster accountability and commitment in the sales person over the longer term. We advocate defining various sets of measures rather than establishing targets against one single figure. Targets and decisions based on a single figure, often involve a number of assumptions that may lead to misleading results. However, CLV is still recognised as a useful approach, so we now show an approach to calculate it.

HOW TO MANAGE THE VALUE OF YOUR CUSTOMERS?

One of the main drawbacks of calculating the customer life value (CLV) is the cost and complexity that obtaining accurate figures often involve. It is advisable to engage in CLV calculations if the process as well as the outcome, are used to inform elements of the customer management strategy such as segmentation and prioritisation. CLV analyses are often undertaken by marketing and finance rather than field sales forces. There are sometimes limitations to what sales people can do to influence the value of their customers in the long term.

Following in this section we present our customer development framework which can be implemented without having to calculate detailed customer financials. Just by analysing the customer lifetime formula, sales executives can identify the four levers or drivers through which a sales person can increase the value of their customer. These drivers are:

1. enhancing cash flows by selling more;
2. enhancing cash flows by reducing costs;
3. accelerating cash flows by reducing the length of the sales process
4. reducing the risks associated with the customer's cash flows.

For each of these drivers several customer development practices exist that we will now present in more detail.

1 SELLING MORE

2 REDUCE COSTS

3 REDUCE RISK

4 ACCELERATE CASH FLOWS

$$\textbf{\textit{Customer Life Time Value}} = \sum_{t=1}^{T} \frac{(\ \text{Revenues}_t\ -\ \text{Costs}_t\ )}{(\ 1+\ \text{risk}\ )^{\text{time}}}$$

1
SELLING MORE

ENHANCING CASH FLOWS BY **SELLING MORE**

Selling more basically refers to finding ways to increase the share of wallet of the customer's total spending on your product or service category. Knowing the customer's share of wallet provides the supplier with an insight to evaluate the strength of the relationship with the customer. Increasing the share of a customer's wallet is often a more cost effective way of boosting revenue than increasing market share. A supplier can increase its cash flows by:

1. SELLING MORE TO EXISTING USERS
2. SELLING MORE TO NEW USERS,
3. CROSS-SELLING OTHER PRODUCTS AND SERVICES,
4. INVITING THE CUSTOMER TO CO-CREATE THEIR VALUE PROPOSITION,
5. SELL A FULLY INTEGRATED SOLUTION.

1. SELLING MORE TO EXISTING USERS

Selling more to current users means displacing one of your main competitors in the customer.

HOW TO DISLODGE AN EXISTING SUPPLIER AND TAKE OVER THEIR REVENUES?

To increase their share of wallet, sales people tend to rely on developing good and close relationships with their customers and on ensuring they are satisfied. While these tactics are effective at maintaining and securing existing business, they are less effective at winning more business and displacing the competition. Remember they too are developing relationships with the customer. To win more business you need to uncover who else the customer is working with, what your rank is relative to your competitors and why; review the reasons why your customer is also doing business with your competitors and see how you could address them, what the cost would be and what the potential financial gains are likely to be. We often see that sales people are reluctant to ask for this type of information from their customers. For customers, unless they perceive clear benefits of disclosing this info, they will be reluctant to do so. One of the ways to circumvent these difficulties is to include questions related to the competition in customer satisfaction surveys. These enquiries often have as its ultimate objective to improve the quality of service delivery, thus, the customer may reveal their expectations from suppliers. Increasing your share of wallet is desirable but not always possible. For instance, many large organisations have reduced their number of IT suppliers to a shortlist of four or five. The IT contracts are divided amongst these suppliers using a set of criteria based on the customer's perception of the supplier's core competencies. The aim for the customer is to keep each of their suppliers sufficiently happy by allocating enough work to each of them in order to maintain the level of service received. The other objective for the customer is not to become overly dependent on any one supplier.

Getting a bigger share of customer's wallet!

When suppliers are fighting amongst each other to get a larger part of the customer's wallet, it often makes the customer's task of managing suppliers very difficult. We have known of cases where trying to increase the share of wallet resulted in a supplier being removed from their customer's short lists. It is, therefore, essential to understand the reasons why a customer also works with your competitors. If one of the reasons is intentionally to divide the work across several suppliers, this has to be taken into account in the business development strategy with that customer.

2. SELLING MORE TO NEW USERS

A sales person can enhance his/her company's sales revenues by selling more of the current products and services to new users such as other business units or other geographical locations within the same customer organisation.

HOW TO FIND THESE NEW USERS WITHIN THE CUSTOMER'S ORGANIZATION?

There is not a single way to increase the reach and influence within the customer organisation as this is customer specific. A good example is provided by LMS, a Belgian software and engineering provider, that offers solutions for the automotive, aerospace and other advanced manufacturing industries. They provide a unique set of simulation and testing systems for engineers involved in research and development. These large global organisations often start by using LMS's technology within one subsidiary in one country. The challenge for LMS's sales people consists of finding other potential users amongst all their customer's subsidiaries around the world. Their sales process is characterised by protracted time frames and often expensive. One approach they have adopted with these large organisations is to offer them an assessment service. By allowing LMS to assess and benchmark all the departments, which could benefit from their technology the customer obtains a global overview of where in their organisation they can improve the efficiency of their operations. To do that they need to supply LMS with access to all the departments within their organisations who are involved in research and development activities. LMS uses the insights derived from the assessment to propose their service to relevant individuals and organizations.

Through this service LMS gets:
• access to all the areas within their customer's operations where their products and services can be of value.
• an overview of the potential added value they could bring to each of the users

3. CROSS SELLING OTHER PRODUCTS AND SERVICES

By cross-selling or up-selling other products and services, revenues can be increased. This approach refers to selling additional services to the existing offering or by selling products and services, which address other problems and needs of the customer. This also enhances customer loyalty and often increases the cost of switching between suppliers. A long-standing challenge for product-oriented sales forces is fostering cross selling of products or services from different business units. Organisations typically start by introducing new tools to exchange information and leads, and new incentive systems to encourage these exchanges.

HOW TO PROMOTE CROSS SELLING ACTIVITIES AMONG EN EXISTING SALES FORCE?

One large financial organisation we had access to saw an increase in their cross selling only after the introduction of account managers being held responsible for selling the bank's whole product and service portfolio. At the start of the year, each account manager had to include in their sales plan which products and services they were going to introduce to their customers. This was done in collaboration with the product sales people who lobbied all the account managers to promote their products or services to their accounts. The system worked because in order for the product sales people to reach their targets they had to collaborate with the account managers who worked across business units and vice versa. The introduction of account managers together with a system of mutual dependency between all the sales people meant they were more focused on raising their levels of cross selling. The existing CRM system became a supporting tool to register and follow up on the agreed actions between the account managers and the product sales forces. In this occasion the CRM system was no longer seen as a control mechanism by the sales forces but rather as a tool to help them to keep track of what was agreed and to follow up what needed to be done.

1
SELLING MORE

2
REDUCE COSTS

3
ACCELERATE CASH FLOW

4
REDUCE RISK

4. INVITE THE CUSTOMER TO CO-CREATE THEIR VALUE PROPOSITION

Many suppliers across many industries are witnessing the trend whereby certain customers want to get involved during the research, development and even marketing of their products. The process relies on a meaningful interaction and dialogue between the customer and the supplier requiring both access to knowledge and transparency of information. In return, customers will also bear more responsibility for dealing with the risks associated with the co-creation process. Prahalad and Ramaswamy, conceptualised the co-creation process in a model called the DART (for dialogue, access, risk-benefits, transparency)[6].

According to their model sales people could add value to their customers by:
• enhancing the *dialogue*, which means more than listening to the customer but involves sharing information and learning's across the whole co-creation process with the customer but also with other parties involved;
• ensuring that all parties involved in the process have complete *access* to all the necessary information and tools;
• ensuring that all parties are fully aware and accept the *risks* associated with the co-creation process;
• ensuring *transparency* between all parties involved.

HOW TO USE CO-CREATION AS A SALES METHODOLOGY?

We have covered the co-creation approach in detail in previous chapters. Here we refer to a case that illustrates this in practice. It is the experience of one research and development organisation that regularly develops or updates their vision of where they see new technologies evolving in the coming years. Their vision is expressed in the form of technology roadmaps, which they then use to align their research and development projects. The roadmaps enable the organisation to align the type of internal capabilities they need with the type of research projects they will be looking for in the market. For the sales people these roadmaps are much more than a vision. They are sales tools through which they can create a meaningful dialogue with their customers about the future of their industry. By providing their customers and prospects with access to their roadmaps, the sales people hope that the customer will open up and share their own vision of the future. This process allows both the sales person and the customer to find areas for co-creation. It also provides a regular validation of their roadmap for the future.

5. SELL A FULLY INTEGRATED SOLUTIONS

Many manufacturers have started offering various services on top of their product in order to differentiate themselves and avoid being viewed as a commodity. Organisations such as Ericsson, Rolls Royce, Siemens and IBM, among many others, offer their customers a wide type of consulting, system integration, financing, maintenance and repair services. Instead of just up selling or cross-selling products these services are offered as an integrated solution, often in combination with products to their customer. For sales people this means a dramatic shift from selling discrete products and/or services to selling complete and integrated value propositions.

One example of innovative product-service offering is Rolls-Royce, the global aerospace, marine and energy engineering company. Their offering goes beyond selling aero engines to airlines and aircraft manufacturers, to provide them with "Power by the Hour" solution (see chapter 1). Their customers pay for the use of the engine through a special financing solution that automatically integrates the engine's maintenance and repair services. In order to enhance the delivery of this solution Rolls-Royce has developed real-time monitoring systems for the engines. While this allows them to anticipate when an engine needs to be serviced it also provides them with valuable data on how the engine performs in various flying conditions. This knowledge enables Rolls-Royce to provide their customers with new services such as advise on operating the engines in order to optimise fuel consumption and to maximise the engines' lifetime. This exemplifies how selling integrated solutions offers new business opportunities based on the new knowledge and capabilities developed by the supplier.

Offering integrated solutions is not only an option in mature markets it can also offer a route to market for new emerging technologies. Like other traditional industries where technology is opening new operational models, the graphical printing market is going through difficult times. Global demand for printed material is diminishing and prices are collapsing. One equipment reseller active in this sector decided to diversify by entering the 3D market space. Beside the problems of maintaining, operating and financing these systems, potential buyers are still wondering about how the market will evolve and which type of applications will be successful. This has a significant effect on the uptake of these new systems. As a result, the organisation decided to provide their potential customers with an integrated managed service solution. By offering to manage the system on behalf of their customers, they would provide their customers a fully integrated solution ranging from web shop integration through to the printing and delivery of the final product. This allows their customers to focus only on finding the right opportunity and building the right business model without requiring an initial upfront investment.

2

REDUCING COSTS

ENHANCING CASH FLOWS BY REDUCING COSTS

LET THE CUSTOMER PERFORM CERTAIN PARTS OF THE PROCESS

Costs can be reduced by improving the efficiency of internal processes or by leveraging external resources, such as involving the customers in certain parts of the value creation process.

Partnering and co-creation can be used in a way that may result in lower R&D costs. One of the benefits of co-creation is the ability to benefit from the innovative capabilities of the customer. Boeing consulted and involved airlines extensively towards the final design of its latest aircraft, the B787 (Dreamliner). One well-known example is IKEA. Normally, a furniture store will deliver the new furniture your home, ready to be used. At IKEA the customer carries the costs of transporting and assembling the furniture. We may not think about it in these terms but in order to use the furniture you buy at IKEA you have to co-create it. The same is true in our supermarkets. Although we may perceive self-scanning as an added value we are actually engaged in a co-creation by taking over part of the work of the supermarket.

Business organisations sometimes involve the customer in co-financing new product developments. Rolls-Royce entered into partnership agreements with Airbus prior to the development of the Trent XWB engine, developed specifically for the Airbus A350. One European manufacturing organisation decided that they would no longer develop new innovative products on their own. Instead, innovations would have to be done in close collaboration with, and co-funded by a customer. Sometimes this approach responds to the requirements of just one customer. In other cases, this is used as a mechanism to develop capabilities that may be used again for another customer. Suppliers need to understand the costs of developing fully customised solutions; these solutions are often resource-intensive and the profits doubtful. In other cases, suppliers engage the customers in co-creation as a mechanism to develop capabilities that may be used again for another customer.

3

ACCELERATE CASH FLOWS

ENHANCING CASH FLOWS BY ACCELERATING CASH FLOWS

To understand how suppliers can accelerate cash flows one needs to look at the factors that affect the time scales in the customer's purchasing process.

1. The more people are involved in the purchasing process, the more complex it will be and the longer it will take.

2. The less familiar an organisation is buying your products the longer the buying process.

3. The larger the investments or the change required utilising your product/service the longer the buying process.

4. The more information that needs to be processed the longer the purchasing process.

New and complex purchase decisions require the customer to analyse and process a lot of information in order to make an informed purchase decision. Let us look at different sales strategies that could adopt to address these issues:

1. UPGRADE YOUR SELLING APPROACH
2. START SMALL, PROPOSE A PROOF OF CONCEPT OR A PILOT
3. SELL IT AS A SERVICE
4. COACH THE BUYING PROCESS

1. UPGRADE YOUR SALES APPROACH

One approach is to sell your products and services to individuals higher up in the organisation's hierarchy. Often in a business-to-business context, the person or department who experiences a problem is not the same as the person or department who can make the purchase decision. Often, committees or groups are commissioned to make a purchasing decision, and thus, they have to analyse the problem and proposed solutions in order to make such purchase decision. One way to shortening the closing of business opportunities is to sell higher into the customer organisational hierarchy. Often, the higher a person is in the hierarchy the more authority they have to make purchase decisions or to influence one. By focusing the sales effort on demonstrating how the supplier's products and services can solve the customer problems beyond purely operational needs, account managers may be able to enlist the support of senior executives, and in so doing shorten their sales cycle.

Thus how can a seller influence senior managers? IBM provides an interesting example, with the annual CEO study, conducted by sales staff with senior officers about trends and strategic issues affecting their businesses. Anyone who has an email address has probably been invited to participate in a survey on a specific business topic. Most of us do not participate anymore these days given the saturation of unsolicited surveys, which makes it very difficult for research and consulting organisation to create reliable benchmark databases. IBM for their CEO survey uses a different approach. They collect their data using face-to-face interviews, which give a sales person the opportunity to have a meeting with senior executives with whom they would not normally interact. As the meeting is about the customer's views and opinions and not about the seller's product and services it is also more likely to result in a good atmosphere than if it was a sales call. Based on the rapport developed during the first interview the sales person has the opportunity to return to their customers and present the results. By presenting the customer's opinions and beliefs alongside those of other organisations, the seller can objectively challenge the customer's view. This process requires a constructive dialogue based on trust and has intrinsic value for both the customer and the seller. As a result the seller can offer some services such as a feasibility or assessment service to help further investigate certain issues and offers advice on how best to approach them.

Another approach to enhance the chances of selling your products and services in complex procurement settings is to "get in" early in the customer's purchasing process, typically well before the invitation to tender is issued. The earlier the sales person gets into the process the more they are able to influence the supplier selection criteria and the package's specifications to their advantage. In recent years, sales organisations have started focusing on the business issues of their customers first,

1
SELLING
MORE

2
REDUCE
COSTS

3
ACCELERATE
CASH FLOW

4
REDUCE
RISK

then translating these into specific needs, and then matching the relevant elements of these issues to the supplier's products and services. It is often referred to as going beyond your product or services and understanding how you can help the customer achieve their own objectives. It is also called focusing on the customer's customers. For instance if your customer is an IT department then their customers are the other departments within their organisation. By helping the IT department find ways to better service their internal department, a supplier demonstrates superior value. Such suppliers will be aware of new IT need long before anybody else placing them in a good position to win the new business opportunities.

THE QUESTION IS HOW TO FIND WHICH TYPE OF SERVICES YOU CAN OFFER YOUR CUSTOMERS TO ADD MORE VALUE AND BE INVOLVED EARLY ON IN THEIR PURCHASING PROCESS?

MLP is a leading German financial institution. As an independent broker, it is MLP's vision to provide discerning clients with integrated financial services and to become the best partner for them at every stage of their lives for services such as pension, asset management and risk management[8]. MLP's focus is on distinct professional groups, such as doctors and lawyers, economists and scientists, IT-specialists, engineers and academics, who the company believes have high future earning potential and attractive risk profiles. Its main clients are university-educated men and women whom the firm has served since their graduation. In order to ensure their clients are successful, the organisation offers a number of services in order to help them. For instance, young graduates are helped by preparing them for recruitment tests and job interviews. When a self-employed person wants to sell their practice, MLP will search for a suitable candidate thereby acting as a broker. By having a specific industry focus the financial advisors also have a specific network and insight in the market. This enables them to provide their customers with career advice and even help them make the next career step. MLP believes that by focusing on making the customer successful they in turn will become successful in a sort of win-win relationship.

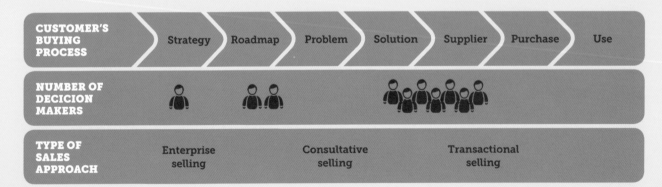

CUSTOMER'S BUYING PROCESS	Strategy	Roadmap	Problem	Solution	Supplier	Purchase	Use
NUMBER OF DECICION MAKERS							
TYPE OF SALES APPROACH	Enterprise selling		Consultative selling		Transactional selling		

Adapted from Neil Rackham and John Devincentis, 1999, "Rethinking the Sales Force"

2. START SMALL: PILOT PROJECT

By allowing the customer to test your product in a pilot project may help them to get more familiar with your offering. Bekaert the a global leader in the development and production of metallic wire-based materials use this approach with some of its customers in the manufacture of many different types of products around the world. In the building and construction sectors, Bekaert manufactures high performance reinforcement products for simplifying construction with applications in masonry, rendering, and concrete. The concrete reinforcement products Dramix® are an alternative to mesh which is the conventional approach for concrete reinforcement. Therefore, these products require a considerable amount of sales effort to educate, promote and introduce them in each specific market. The products are distributed directly to building contractors. Sales people are mainly focusing their activities on educating prescribers, selling to building contractors and managing relationships with distributors. Their work is highly centred on identifying and developing business opportunities. They maintain close relationships with architect and engineering companies enabling them to identify potential opportunities early on. Once a potential opportunity is identified with the help of the technical managers, they assist the engineering companies with the technical calculation and design work. This may involve tests to prove the efficacy of Bekaert's products as opposed to the conventional reinforcement techniques. Once their products and technology is, prescribe the sales person has to convince the building constructor to use their products and technology for this project as opposed to the conventional methods they are used to. This, again, will require the involvement of the technical managers. However, the perceived risk of using this new method may be too high for a building constructor to take. For that reason Bekaert also has a special insurance solution, which allows them to take over the initial risk. To achieve profitable growth it is essential for Bekaert that engineers and contractors, once using the product on a pilot project and experiencing the benefits, keep on acquiring and using the product.

129

MESH

FIBER

3. START SMALL: PROOF OF CONCEPT PROJECT

If the pilot test does not suit your value proposition why not offer a proof of concept. This enables the customers to see how the value proposition will work and how they may be likely to benefit from it. The speed and the rise of technology in business have led many organisations to invest heavily in all kinds of new technologies in order not to lose out on a new business opportunity. Decisions were often made based on some slides claiming the marvellous benefits the organisation would reap by adopting some new technology. However, many suppliers in the IT sector notice that customers are becoming much more critical and no longer agree to make large investments based on a set of slides. As one integrator told us "you have to show them the money".

CGI a large IT consulting organisation, has introduced innovation centres called SPARK centres organised by themes around different locations in the world. The idea is that customers no longer have to learn about new ideas and technology through slides but can come to the centres and touch and feel the new technologies and see how they could help in solving their business problems. CGI organises workshops for their customers in their SPARK centres to experience new technologies and brainstorm on how these could help spark new business applications. The ability to touch and feel new technologies

creates a positive experience generating trust and openness needed to have a dialogue and co-create new applications. The brainstorm often leads to new ideas of applications the customer can use this new technology for. This leads to small proof of concept type projects. These are relatively small projects offering the ability to test the new technology and its application. If it works the customer initiate the proper budgeting procedure in order to implement the new idea as part of a full-scale project.

This approach of developing innovation together with the customer using a proof of concept as a starting point offer the following benefits:

1. It enables a quick sale by keeping the proposal small as a proof of concept. Executives can decide on such projects without needing committees to review the proposal.

2. Proof of concepts allow CGI to be well positioned to also win the larger implementation deal if the proof of concepts is successful

3. It provides a means for CGI to promote itself as an innovative organisation which will enhance their brand value in the eyes of their customers.

4. START SMALL: TROJAN HORSE

A third approach consists of offering a "Trojan Horse". This is a limited module of the whole value proposition for the customer to become better acquainted with the system and what it can mean for them. If you want to dislodge an established supplier of a customer you need to think about your sales strategy carefully. You can attack them head on by demonstrating how your solution is superior to theirs. However, this is a very difficult sale as you have to convince a customer that the investment they already made was not the best and that they have to invest again in your solution. There is going to be a lot of internal resistance and the existing supplier is not going to take it lying down either. It is often said that you need to have a 3 to 1 advantage if you want to take this approach. In other words, you need a very strong business case to win. Another approach is to ignore the established supplier and provide modules or pieces of your solutions to one part of the customer's business. ERP vendors often sell module by module instead of the complete suite of products. They first sell a module of their software to, for instance, the HR department. Then they focus on the marketing department and build step by step their reputation until the moment where they can sell the complete suite of products. Their key argument is the benefit the organisation can obtain by linking all these modules together into one single solution. As soon as this starts it becomes very difficult for any organisation to drop the solutions as it has become too integrated into their business processes.

3. SELL IT AS A SERVICE

By selling your product as a service, your customers only pay when they use the product or service thereby reducing the upfront investment and allowing it to be booked as operational expenditure. This also reduces the customer risk associated with the purchase decision. This involves value-based pricing which is based on either the quantity of the product or service used or on the quality of the customer's outcomes. Quantity-based pricing is based on subscriptions whereby the customer pays a fixed sum on a regular basis. For example, online software providers charge their customers a monthly subscription fee for the use of their software. It can also be based on utility- based pricing whereby the customer pays an amount based on the actual use of the product. For example, manufacturers of copier machines have since long offered their customers 'pay per copy' schemes to avoid making upfront investments, but instead paying depending on usage.

Quality or outcome- based agreements are approaches aimed to add more value to the customers by offering relevant guarantees and gain sharing alternatives. Fixed fee and fixed outcome-based pricing is effectively a risk-sharing proposal whereby the supplier guarantees the complete project will not overrun a specific price. Consulting organisations often invoice on a time and material basis. However, their customers also need to budget the overall investment they are going to make. Often, agreements are made such that the overall project will not overrun the agreed budgets. The consulting organisation therefore accepts a large part of the project risk on behalf of the customer.

Gain sharing pricing is based on the level of value the customer generates from the solution. Sometimes relationships between a supplier and their customer reach a level whereby they agree to form a joint venture in which each takes a part of the investment costs but they will take a part of the overall benefits as well. The main problem with gain sharing is agreeing on set business targets and ways of measuring them. The complexity involved often outweighs the benefits of such deals. Alternatively, some organisations we interviewed were looking into ways to link their invoice amounts to their customer satisfaction levels. The idea is that a part of the invoice is based on the customer's satisfaction of the supplier's service.

VALUE BASED PRICING MECHANISMS FOR SOLUTIONS

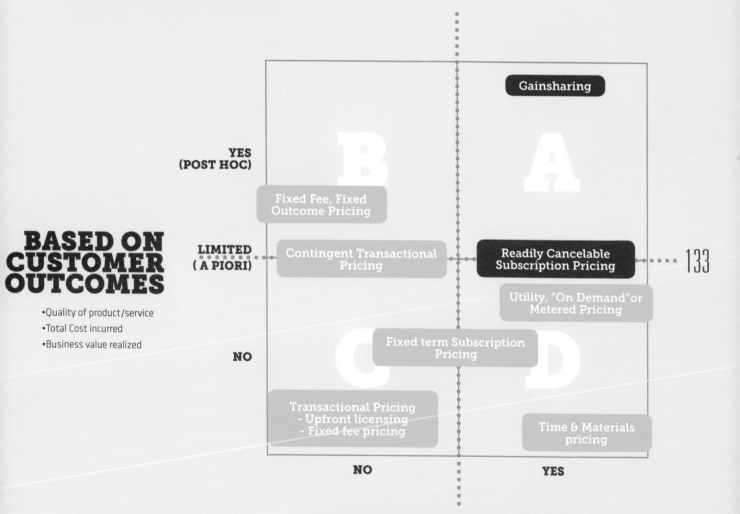

BASED ON CUSTOMER OUTCOMES

- Quality of product/service
- Total Cost incurred
- Business value realized

YES (POST HOC)

LIMITED (A PIORI)

NO

B

A

C

D

Gainsharing

Fixed Fee, Fixed Outcome Pricing

Contingent Transactional Pricing

Readily Cancelable Subscription Pricing

Utility, "On Demand" or Metered Pricing

Fixed term Subscription Pricing

Transactional Pricing
- Upfront licensing
- Fixed fee pricing

Time & Materials pricing

NO   YES

BASED ON PRODUCT/ SERVICE USAGE

- Volume
- Frequency
- Duration

133

Source: Mohanbir Sawhney, 2004, "Going Beyond the Product: Defining, Designing and Delivering Customer Solutions", published in Robert F. Lusch, Stephen L, 2006,

4. COACH THE BUYING PROCESS

The sales person can coach the buying process by providing some information that the customers can use to help them to make their decision. Professional buyers and customers aim to prepare themselves before a meeting with a sales person. This preparation requires gathering information and insights. Thus, why not provide them with information and tools to conduct fact finding as efficiently as possible?

Engels NV is a family-owned organisation producing, distributing and reselling windows and doors. They offer a complete solution for all types of windows and doors in PVC, aluminium and wood. A few years ago, they started reselling their products through a franchised network of shops. They soon discovered that, for consumers, deciding which materials, options, and colours is a difficult and often very technical challenge. For the consumer, this is not something they purchase regularly and therefore they lack experience and knowledge. Engels NV recognised that, as part of their service offering, they needed to assist their customers. Because the investment amounts are relatively high, people do tend to shop around. However, the proposals and the advice they receive vary from shop to shop making it very complicated for the customer to make a decision. As a result, they developed a purchasing tool in the form of a brochure helping the customer to structure their thoughts and helping them to define their own needs in terms of the type, style, colour, etc. of the windows and doors they need. By helping their customers to clearly define their needs and to translate them into requirements, they helped the customer shorten their decision time. The approach is not to sell but to help the customer to buy.

Customers who buy complex offerings often need to change or realign they organisational structures and processes to extract the maximum value out the suppliers' offer and capabilities. In addition, customers may find it difficult to implement complex solutions by themselves. Thus the question is not so much how to sell but how to motivate your customer to implement new changes, which will facilitate they purchase to fulfil their need for your services or products.

5. ... AND GET PAID FOR IT

One approach to facilitate the customer's management of change is to develop a methodology which is packaged as a service and which will help customers to start implementing the new vision defined by the executives. Several large IT consulting organisations offer their customers a boot camp location together with a methodology to help to go from idea to implementation plan in just a few days. This is also consistent with the co-creation approach because the customer brings its knowledge and ideas and the seller brings its methodologies and location. The combination leads them to co-create the implementation plan together. From the seller's perspective, this approach has the benefit that the customer pays for the boot camp service which otherwise would be a long and costly consultative selling process. The seller is also well placed to propose their additional services and products to help with the implementation.

This approach actually results in reduced sales costs by transforming some of the selling activities into a paid consulting activity. The same approach can also be used by offering quality audits or assessments to customers, to help them pinpoint areas for improvement in their business.

4
REDUCE RISK

ENHANCING CASH FLOWS BY REDUCING RISKS

1. REDUCING RISKS BY BUILDING RELATIONSHIPS

The more stable and predictable the business, the less volatile the cash flows. From a sales perspective, it is all about creating strong and stable customer relationships. These relationships enable an accurate and stable business forecasting process. Focusing on retaining existing customers rather than acquiring new ones also reduces the volatility of the costs. Increasing customer's satisfaction and loyalty also reduces the vulnerability of cash flows. The more customers are satisfied with the organisation's value proposition the less likely they are to switch to a competitor. Loyalty creates a significant barrier to entry for competitors into your customer base. Loyalty is often the result of both, consistent delivery and close business relationships with customers. In customer – supplier relationships different stages can be identified, each of them associated with different levels of intimacy and closeness in the dyad.

EXPLORATORY
This is typically called the prospecting phase where the selling company has identified the organisation as having key account potential. During this stage information is exchanged between the organisations building up the relationship until the moment when the purchase opportunity emerges.

BASIC
Often at this stage, the selling company received a limited order probably for a trial period expecting the selling company to prove itself.

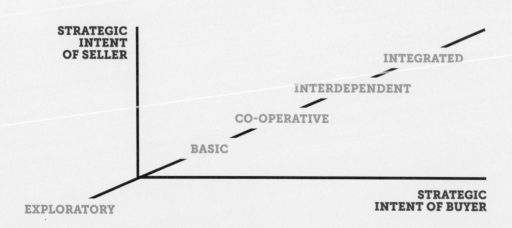

Source: Diana Woodburn, Malcolm McDonald, 2011, Key Account Management: The Definitive Guide, Wiley

1
SELLING
MORE

2
REDUCE
COSTS

3
ACCELERATE
CASH FLOW

4
REDUCE
RISK

CO-OPERATIVE

The goal at this stage is to become the preferred supplier. The key account manager must seek out the areas within the buyer's company where the competitors are active. During this stage, the key account manager and the purchase manager facilitate relationships between the companies at the different levels and departments.

INTERDEPENDENT

During this phase, the key account manager works together with the buying company to develop long- term plans. Plans for new products that are under development are shared with the customers. This is part of normal business as all departments are now directly communicating with each other. The close relationship should enable both companies to lower their costs and to work together and enable the selling company to improve the quality of the products and services.

INTEGRATED

This is the ultimate stage of the relationship where both the buying and the selling company work together almost in complete integration.

At this stage, both companies develop jointly new business plans, strategies and market research. The focus of both companies is to further improve all aspects of them doing business together.

The model describes the different stages of the relationship as an evolutionary sequence. Not all relationships develop all the way through to integrated relationships nor is it the ambition for the supplier or the customer to do so. The nature of the relationship is dependent not only on an organisation's willingness to develop a relationship but also on the nature of the exchanges (simple vs. complex) between the customer and the supplier.

The escalation in stages also illustrates a move from personal to professional or business relationships. Evolving from one form of collaboration to the other requires different degrees of interdependence, trust, joint planning, dedicated teams and multi-level contacts. The following tool helps the analysis of the nature of a particular relationship and helps account managers to gauge at what stage of the relationship they are with their customer.

HOW TO MEASURE THE RELATIONSHIP?

	1 Strongly Disagree	2 Disagree	3 Agree	4 Strongly Agree
Both companies would find ending our relationship difficult and complicated.				
There is a real spirit of partnership and trust between our two companies.				
Together we have produced long-term strategic plans for the development of our relationship.				
Both companies have set up cross functional teams of people dedicated to meeting the customers' needs.				
People at all level in the organisation are in constant communication with each other.				
Both companies acknowledge that the other is important to them.				
Total				

SCORE	RELATIONSHIP STAGE
6 – 10	BASIC
11 – 16	COOPERATIVE
17 – 22	INTERDEPENDENT
23 – 24	INTEGRATED

Source: Diana Woodburn, Malcolm McDonald, 2011, Key Account Management: The Definitive Guide, Wiley

1
SELLING
MORE

2
REDUCE
COSTS

3
ACCELERATE
CASH FLOW

4
REDUCE
RISK

2. REDUCING RISKS BY COLLABORATING

These relationship levels are defined by the frequency of interaction, the depth of the interactions and their scope. The more people from both the seller and the customer organisation communicate with each other over a wide range of issues, the higher the more likely a high level of intimacy will develop. Customers who buy more, more frequently and across different categories are more likely to have better relationships with their suppliers. While selling across different categories will help to build relationships, so will selling across different departments or business units within a single customer. The customer's switching costs increases with multiple relationships with the same supplier. When these relationships are satisfactory and frequent they lead to a greater level of trust, which again leads to longer and more intimate customer supplier relationships.

One of the most important elements in developing these relationships is that the roles of the sales person and the purchasing officer change from being the main points of contacts towards a role as facilitator, helping people of both organisations to work together.

BOW TIE MODEL

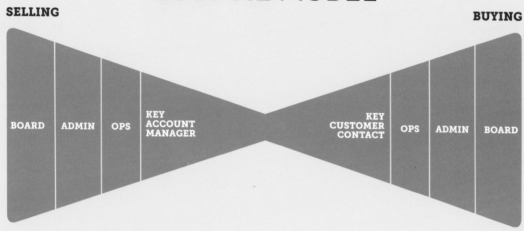

SELLING

BUYING

BOARD | ADMIN | OPS | KEY ACCOUNT MANAGER

KEY CUSTOMER CONTACT | OPS | ADMIN | BOARD

DIAMOND MODEL

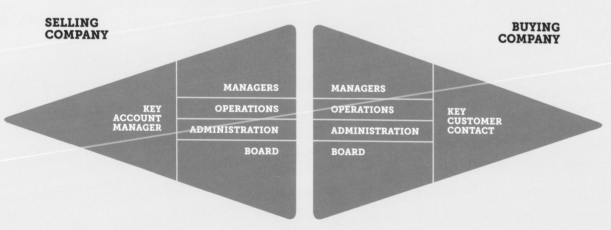

SELLING COMPANY

BUYING COMPANY

KEY ACCOUNT MANAGER

MANAGERS
OPERATIONS
ADMINISTRATION
BOARD

MANAGERS
OPERATIONS
ADMINISTRATION
BOARD

KEY CUSTOMER CONTACT

SUMMARY

Historically most applications of CLV are focused on segmenting customers and allocating resources accordingly. This raises the question: "What is the value of calculating the CLV for an account manager who only manages a few key accounts?" Calculating the profitability and CLV of key accounts is only useful if account managers use them to manage and to inform their decisions about these accounts. In our view, the value lies in the insight gained by the analysis of the CLV and its direct and indirect drivers. Our experience of working with supplier organisations shows that as part of the key account planning, suppliers generally take into account key components of CLV. However, very few go as far as to actually calculate a single value for CLV. Reasons adduced are often that the benefits of calculating CLV reside in the 'process' rather than on the figure itself. Thus, we further developed an account development framework linking all the financial and non-financial drivers of CLV. We have developed this framework as a tool to help strategic account managers to analyse their accounts and to decide the customers with whom they want to engage in co-creation.

CUSTOMER RELATIONSHIPS AND CO-CREATION

In the previous chapter, we mentioned that in almost all the cases where customers and suppliers co-create there is pre-existing relationship. This means that before co-creating with customers, sales people need to build professional relationships.
The table below summarises the different approaches discussed in this chapter but categorized into selling and co-creating approaches.

The table below summarises the different approaches discussed in this chapter but categorized into selling and co-creating approaches.

	increase revenue	reduce costs	reduce risk by building better relationships	accelerate cash flows
STAGE 1 SELLING APPROACH	Selling more to existing users Selling to new users Cross Sell additional products	Seek for ways to reduce internal costs	Explore Relationship Stage Basic Relationship Stage Co-operation Stage	Sell a Pilot Project Sell a Trojan Horse Module
STAGE 2 CO-CREATION APPROACH	Co-Create solutions with the customer Sell it as a service	Offset some costs to the customer	Interdependent Stage Aligned Stage	Make a Proof of Concept with the customer Coach the Buying Process

STAGE 1
SELLING APPROACH

The first stage in a new customer-supplier relationship is to get to know each other. The customer is likely to be focused on understanding how much value can the supplier bring to her/his business. The supplier analyses how profitable the customer could be. At first, the supplier has to build an initial relationship with the customer and has to explore how they could work together. After this exploration phase the sales person present the capabilities and products of her/his organisation and tries to find a possible first opportunity to show the customer what they can do. Such an opportunity is often a pilot project in a specific department of the customer. Through this project, the supplier is able to proof the capability and potential for adding value to the customer. During this stage, the sales person looks for opportunities for additional revenues by selling more of their products to the same users or to different users in the organisation. Using an incremental approach, it may help the sales person to influence more than one part of the customer organization thereby selling to new users within the same organisation. In order to become an established supplier the sales person may need to cross-sell additional products and services. Higher volumes of business need to be made compatible with healthy profit potential. The sales person must analyse the costs of the services offered and the price of the products sold in order to find ways to improve their margin. At this level, the sales person is likely to have achieved the status of an established supplier at a profitable customer.

STAGE 2

CO-CREATION APPROACH

In order to develop a deeper relationship with the customer, the supplier must show how they can add value to the customer's business beyond the products and services delivered or exchanged. At this stage, the sales person looks for ways to involve the customer in co-creating new value propositions with them. This is achieved by learning as much as possible about the customer's 'job to be done' and by finding ways to help the customer in areas with the potential to create superior value. The sales person's job is to demonstrate to the customer that they have the capabilities required to jointly co-create new solutions which will deliver value beyond what they already have.

This can start small with a proof of concept leading to a larger project and full scale implementation. At this stage, the supplier and the customer often become interdependent, as they need each other's capabilities to develop these new solutions. From hereon the customer and the supplier may become partners or even evolve towards the supplier taking over some of the customer processes in the form of managed services. At this stage both parties need to be fully aligned and the main job of the sales person is to ensure that the relationship remains profitable.

EXAMPLE: HOW TO CALCULATE THE LIFETIME VALUE OF A CUSTOMER?

Let us use an example to illustrate how to calculate the customer lifetime value (CLV). CLV calculations often portray a customer as having only one single stream of revenue which will go on forever. In reality, large accounts often generate many different business opportunities and different revenue streams. Let us assume you are a consulting organisation and you want to calculate the CLV of one of your customers. Currently you have three on-going engagements with this customer which all will end in the near future but at different times. In the meantime, you are in discussion with the customer about two new projects. One of these new opportunities has just been identified and you are still in the process of gathering all the relevant information about it. For the second opportunity, you already submitted a proposal and you are towards the end of the sales process negotiating the final details about the contract.

Based on your current knowledge the revenues for all these projects over the next three years look like:

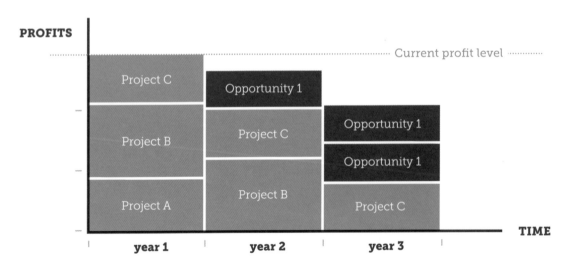

The diagram shows that the current levels of profit cannot be maintained without finding a third new business opportunity which starts in year 2 and goes on in year 3.

THE CLV FORMULA

The calculations of CLV are derived from net present value (NPV) analyses—the NPV of a financial asset is the sum of the discounted future cash flows that are generated from the asset. Similarly, CLV is the NPV of a customer's future profits. CLV is calculated by discounting future cash flows over the lifetime of the customer and can be expressed as:

$$CLV = \sum_{t=1}^{T} \frac{(\text{Cash flow In}_t - \text{Cash flow Out}_t)}{(1+r)^t}$$

Cash Flow In = revenues in time period t
Cash Flow out = costs in time period t
r = discount rate
t = time period
T = the number of time periods for which the CLV is estimated (usually 3 to 5 years)

The example assumes that the revenues will be generated in the next three years. While it is reasonable to assume that relationships between an organisation and its key customers are based on contractual agreements it is not reasonable to assume that therefore all future cash flows are known. Considering this, we first need to calculate net present value (NPV) of each individual business opportunity or contract, taking the purchasing probability into account. The CLV is the sum of the probability-adjusted individual NPVs for the account.

	year 1	year 2	year 3
Project A	100	0	0
Project B	150	150	0
Project C	100	100	100
Opportunity 1	50	50	
Opportunity 2	50		
Total	350	200	200
Discount rate	7,60 %	7,60 %	7,60 %
NPV	325	172	160
CLV	€ 658		

To calculate the NPV of business opportunity we first need to divide the sales process into a number of discrete activities, which represent the purchasing process. Although not all customers follow the same purchasing process, opportunities can be broken down into a set of sequential sales stages ranging from leads to closing the sales. The advantage of the model is that it enables the organisation to break the sales process down into a set of manageable and measurable stages. This helps in gaining visibility and control over what is happening once a prospect is identified.

Having clearly identified each stage of the process, the organisation is able to define clearly which task each sales person must perform, thereby making the whole process more manageable, often a challenge in complex sales processes. The model can be written down into a formula which results can be used for sales forecast purposes.

Several statistical methods exist to calculate the probability a customer will purchase or continue to purchase. In the context of managing key accounts, the knowledge available by the account managers takes precedence over statistical calculations. This method is called scoring, a qualitative way of measuring specific types of probabilities based on the insight available about the chosen accounts and their likely purchase behaviour. Organisations often use scorecards to capture opportunity qualification criteria. These criteria can then be weighted to provide a probability of success. The advantage of this method is that it helps understand what the drivers for winning opportunities are. A simple way of scoring opportunities is to assign probabilities to each stage of the sales process. The total value of the opportunity is multiplied with the probability factor resulting in a forecast value.

$$NPV = \sum_{t=1}^{T} p(Purchase_t) \times \frac{(Cash\ flow\ In_t - Cash\ flow\ Out_t)}{(1+r)^t}$$

Where:
NPV = Net Present Value of an individual project or contract at the customer
p(Purchase) = probability that the customer will purchase or continue to purchase

PROCESS STAGES % PROBABILITY FACTOR	Lead 5%	Prospect 10%	Presentation 25%	Negotiating 50%	Sales 100%

Based on our example we know that Opportunity 1 is already in the negotiation stages while the Opportunity 2 is still in a lead stage. Taking this into account our CLV looks like:

	year 1	year 2	year 3
Project A	100	0	0
Project B	150	150	0
Project C	100	100	100
Opportunity 1		25 (50*50%)	25 (50*50%)
Opportunity 2			2,5 (50*5%)
Total	350	175	127,5
Discount rate	7,60 %	7,60 %	7,60 %
NPV	325	151	102
CLV	€ 658		

HOW TO CALCULATE THE PROBABILITY THAT EXISTING CONTRACTS ARE RENEWED OR THAT THE CUSTOMER WILL CONTINUE TO DO BUSINESS WITH YOU?

For existing contractual business, it is common to take a probability of a 100% for the duration of the contract. The renewal of the contract can be considered as a new opportunity which probability can be defined based on the 'strength of the relationship' between the supplier and the customer. The strength can be measured based on a number of elements such as: longevity of relationship, number of different products/services that are bought, the quality of relationship and the number of contacts between supplier and client (in both directions). This method to assess the strength of a relationship can then be used to inform the customer portfolio strategy matrix[11] , and to be used as a basis to determine the probability of the retention rate.

HOW TO ALLOCATE THE SALES COSTS?

The formula below includes the sales/account management costs as part of the outgoing cash flows. However, a large amount of these costs will be generated regardless of whether the customer purchases or not. Costs related to the acquisition, development and retention of key accounts need to be included in the overall customer lifetime value, given that are 'fixed' costs the supplier incurs in. This raises the question whether to include these key account management costs at the level of the individual project or contract or at the customer level. This depends on how the key account management programme is organised.

In a large matrix organisation such as IBM, you may have dedicated key account managers for specific customers. Their costs can be reasonably attributed at a customer level. However, account managers involve product experts which are sales people working in the specific business units when promoting particular solutions for specific customers. If there is not a specific opportunity account managers are working on, these specialist sales people will not be called upon making their costs generic rather than specific to an individual business opportunity.

The CLV is the sum of all the NPV of all existing and potential projects and contracts minus the costs associated with the development and retaining of the key account.

$$CLV = \sum_{n=1}^{N} NPV_n - \sum_{t=1}^{T} \frac{(KAMCost_t)}{(1+r)^t}$$

Where:
N = number of existing and potential projects and contracts
n = current project or contract
KAMCost = costs of managing the key account as whole

	year 1	year 2	year 3
Project A	100	0	0
Project B	150	150	0
Project C	100	100	100
Opportunity 1		25 (50*50%)	25 (50*50%)
Opportunity 2			2,5 (50*5%)
Minus KAM cost	10	10	10
Total	340	165	117,5
Discount rate	7,60 %	7,60 %	7,60 %
NPV	315	142	94
CLV	€ 552		

Let assume that the overall costs of managing the account are fixed at a value of 10.

Chapter 5
FROM MANAGING TO COLLABORATING

QUESTION:
You have decided to introduce a new CRM system in your sales organisation. How will you motivate the sales people to use it so maximum benefits from the system can be realised?

When considering how to support sales force effectiveness in your sales people's yearly performance review, what do you do? When we ask this question with a group of sales managers, very often the responses relate to either emphasis on the incentives associated with achievement or on the consequences linked to non-achievement. Motivating sales people either through rewards or punishments is deeply ingrained in sales management practices. It is the equivalent of the carrot and stick part of the command and control management approach. This form of sales management relies on breaking the sales process down into a set of manageable tasks, which are believed to be trained, monitored and incentivised. The assumption underlying this view is that sales people, if left unsupervised, make decisions based on self-interest, i.e. "what's in it for me", and hence will make a decision that is not necessarily aligned to the best interest of the business. Before questioning the control-focused paradigm of management, we first need to understand where it came from.

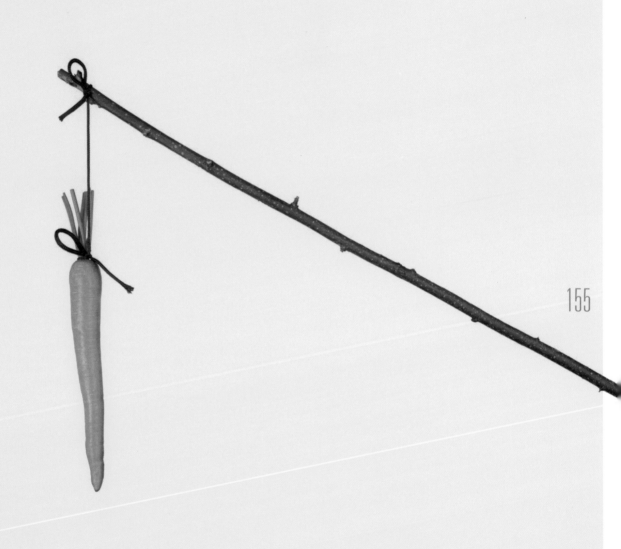

Ancient Greece

Adam Smith

Humans are self interested and that their decisions are driven by rational choice which in a free market will serve a common good.

Henry Ford

Work is best organised using assembly lines based on a tightly controlled management system.

322 BC

1790

1920

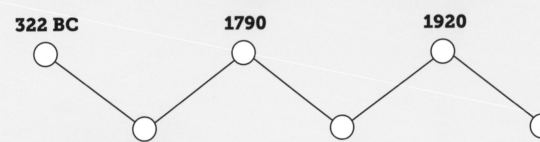

156

1679

Thomas Hobbes

Humans were like wolves to each other and that the role of governments is to control them.

1915

Frederick Taylor

Employees are demotivated and work processes are not well defined.

1944

John Nash

How to make decisions based on rational self-interest theory?

WHAT ARE THE ORIGINS OF MODERN MANAGMENT?

The belief that human beings are predominantly motivated by self-interest goes back to the Greek philosopher, Aristotle. In contrast to Aristotle, Plato was not concerned with self-interest but believed in the principle that in order to create an ideal state people should have everything in common. This difference between Aristotle and Plato, highlights the problem of combining self-interest with the wellbeing of society. According to Tomas Hobbes, a seventeenth century thinker, humans behave like wolves to each other, that is they will 'predate' each other to survive, and the role of governments is to control them to ensure peace and economic development. This is because Hobbes claimed that our pursuit of self-interest would eventually lead to our own downfall. The role of governments is to control our behaviour in order to prevent us from harming ourselves or others. In contrast, eighteenth century thinker Adam Smith had a different view. He provided the foundations of modern economics assuming that humans are self-interested but that their decisions are driven by rational choice which, in a free market, would serve as a common good. With the industrial revolution came the need to incorporate those ideas into the ways factories were managed. Frederik Taylor, the "father" of scientific management, noticed that factory workers were operating well below their full capacity. He attributed this to three causes:

1. workers were not incentivised to work harder;
2. if workers were more productive fewer of them would be needed, hence the fear of losing their job made them less hard working, and,
3. workers wasted a lot of their time on ill-defined working methods: The work relied too much on rule of thumb methods rather than well-defined procedures.

Scientific management for Taylor consisted of analysing and defining the work in great level of detail, breaking processes into specific tasks. Workers would be trained to perform the task according to a set of quality standards and under exhaustive instruction and supervision. These principles led gradually to the widespread use of assembly lines in factories. The system relied on a tightly controlled management system and worked well in the manufacturing environment of the last century. The downside of this approach is that the high levels of control over how the work needs to be performed reduces the system's adaptability and ability to respond flexibly to complexity and uncertainty. Over the past few decades, we have witnessed ever-increasing rates of innovation and change, rendering Taylorism largely ineffective in a number of contexts. In order to develop management systems that could support organisational adaptation and change, management thinking started focusing on finding ways to align employees' self-interests with those of the organisation.

A key approach to align the principal (business owner) with the agent's (managers and workers) interest, are incentive systems. Proponents of agency theory, the concept underpinning extrinsic incentive systems, postulate that people are rational and try to maximise their personal gains. Thus, in order to align individuals' interests with those of their organisations in certain contexts, incentives and punishments need to be established. By carefully designing incentives the behaviours of the employees would be coherent with the objectives of the organisation and the defined work processes. These paradigms later evolved to management by objectives and subsequently derived into new management practices, such as balanced scorecards, and other tools to both align objectives and to motivate employees.

STRENGTHS AND WEAKNESSES OF THE SELF-INTEREST THEORY

Some of the advantages of the self-interest theory (more widely known as agency theory) are that its principles can be translated relatively easily into management tools. Its principles are applicable to a wide range of circumstances with positive effects in the short-term. However, the tenets of agency theory tend to over simplify human behaviour. It ignores the complex nature of work in modern organisations and is unable to account for the volatility and uncertainty of the environment within which businesses operate nowadays. For instance, during the early 1990s evidence showed that people are not only motivated by self-interest. The rise of open source software projects revealed motives beyond the pursuit of extrinsic benefits. Since the new millennium, user-generated content and the formation of user communities' collaborating in areas of common interest have become the norm. According to Yochai Benkler[1], open sources and user-generated content based on collaboration are becoming significant economical production methods, which raises many questions on economic theories based on rational self-interest. In order to understand the motives of individuals to collaborate on projects without any apparent motive for economic gains, one may draw on sociological and anthropological theories. These theories reveal that collaboration and community is an effective mechanism for enhancing competitiveness and survival. Rather than individual direct gains, they facilitate the creation of collective wealth, which in turn may derive in individual benefits. For-profit corporations, are often primarily driven by purely selfish motives such as to maximise profits and shareholder value. Liberal economists have long argued that the rational selfishness of corporations does serve the common good through market self-regulation. However, the last financial crisis (2007-2013) and high profile failures in financial services arguably associated to onerous bonuses has led to a debate questioning whether management systems based on conceptions of individuals' self-interest may destroy rather than create wealth and prosperity and the advancement of societal well-being.

"My question is simple. Were you wrong?"
Congressman **Henry Waxman**

"Partially ... I made a mistake in presuming that the self-interest of organisations, specifically banks, is such that they were best capable of protecting shareholders and equity in the firms ... I discovered a flaw in the model that I perceived is the critical functioning structure that defines how the world works.
..."

Alan Greenspan

159

ARE WE REALLY RATIONAL WHEN MAKING DECISIONS?

One of the most widely accepted theories on human motivation is the 'expectancy theory' developed by Victor Vroom[2]. The theory proposes that people are motivated to exert effort when the results they expect to achieve are linked to a reward they value. Central to this theory are three main concepts:

1. **Expectancy**. This refers to a person's perceived relationship between effort and performance, i.e. the extent to which a person believes that increased effort will lead to higher performance and achievement of certain expected outcomes.
2. **Instrumentality**. This reflects the person's perception of the relationship between performance and reward; for example, it reflects the extent to which a person believes that higher performance will lead to promotion.
3. **Valence**. This represents the value placed upon a particular reward by a person.

Thus, according to Vroom's theory, if a salesperson believes that by working longer hours she/he will achieve increased sales (high expectancy) and that higher sales will lead to greater commission (high instrumentality) and higher commission is important for the person (high valence), a high level of motivation (i.e. willingness to devote extra effort) should result. The picture below shows the nature of the relationship:

| EFFORT | EXPECTANCY | PERFORMANCE | INSTRUMENTALITY | REWARD | VALENCE | VALUE OF REWARD |

e.g. increased call rate, longer working day

e.g. increased sales, increase in numbers of active accounts, higher sales call ratio

e.g. higher pay, sense of accomplishment, respect, promotion

According to Vroom's theory, appropriate training in combination with well-designed reward programmes will result in highly motivated (sales) people who will strive to perform at their best. This assumes people are rational human beings primarily driven by personal benefits maximisation. This belief is consistent with the self-interest theory that prevailed for some decades last century.

Research that is more recent shows that some of the premises on which sales compensation systems are based need to be revised[3]. As individuals we are both rational decision-makers but our behaviour is also largely driven by emotions. We are all familiar with situations in which our emotions override our capacity to reason. For instance, individuals often behave in ways that are driven by emotional well-being and pleasure rather than accomplishment and achievement. It happens when a sales person postpones calling a prospect, hands in their proposal at the very last moment, or when they use the time set aside for working to indulge in something more pleasurable. This process is called procrastination and is about living for the moment whereby we often put off tasks until later knowing that we will be worse off. According to Pierce Steel from the University of Calgary we are all procrastinators[4]. People who procrastinate tend to be highly impulsive and place more value on what they have today versus what they can have tomorrow. Based on his research he developed an equation to calculate the level of people's motivation. The equation consists of the person's expectancy for success at a task; the value of the reward for completing the tasks; the person's degree of impulsiveness; and the person's sensitivity to delay.

$$MOTIVATION = \frac{EXPECTANCY \times VALUE}{IMPULSIVENESS \times DELAY}$$

Impulsiveness is the tendency to act without sufficient deliberation about our actions and their consequences. People who are impulsive, place more value on what they have today versus what they can have tomorrow. This is related to our ability to exercise self-control, which is related to the interplay between reason and emotions. People with high self-control are better able to control their impulses and tend therefore to be less likely to procrastinate.

Many activities we perform during a day are completely automatic such as, how to walk without falling, breathing and even to some extent driving. We seem to run on 'autopilot' without requiring conscious effort. Often when we feel or react impulsively, we are running on 'autopilot'.

When we begin to learn a new activity such as selling a new product or service, we are highly concentrated on our own behaviour, sometimes at the expense of being aware of what is happening around us, such as the reaction of a customer in a sales encounter. Learning new skills requires focused attention. Over time, however as one becomes proficient at a particular task, the behaviour becomes automatic and no longer requires conscious observation. The danger of automatic

responses and why they become so pervasive is that they feel effortless. Many of us approach tasks at work on autopilot. Impulsive behaviours are forms of 'autopilot' behaviour as is procrastination.

Even when people develop careful plans for their work, the tendency to react automatically does not disappear. Sales people make sales plans detailing how they will reach their targets. However, once at work, sales professionals often default to 'known behaviours' when faced with novel challenges, or engage in procrastination of perceived difficult tasks. They put off actions, which have been defined and are part of their sales plan… and compensate this with excessive focus on current customer requests for instance. When confronted with their behaviour they unconsciously adopt a 'justification mode' arguing that they cannot ignore their customers and that they have to deal with them first. If they miss their target it will not be their fault but because managing existing customers takes most of their time. The underpinning phenomenon is that handling existing customers allows the sales people to run on 'autopilot' given that current customers may require comparably less effort to handle. Tackling procrastination is not straightforward or easy for the reasons we describe next.

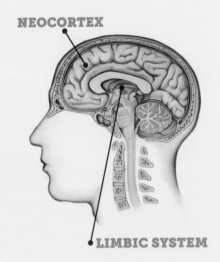

NEOCORTEX

LIMBIC SYSTEM

WE ARE WIRED
TO PROCRASTINATE.

To fully understand human behaviour we need to
look into the two systems that govern the mind:

1. THE RATIONAL MIND located in the neocortex, which is analytical and slow to act, and
2. THE EMOTIONAL MIND located in the limbic system, which is impulsive and more
susceptible to habit. The limbic system is responsible for our emotions. It is based on much
more immediate, or short-term, reactions. Another way to see emotions is as automatic
processes. Automatic processes are responsible for basic functions such as breathing, walking,
etc. The neocortex comprises the frontal lobes of the brain generating our rational thoughts.
It is responsible for the development of human language, abstract thought, imagination,
and consciousness. The neocortex is flexible and has almost infinite learning capacity. This is
where we have our right and left hemispheres. The limbic system is the part of the brain that
was developed in the first place and it is more powerful than the neocortex. The two systems
work in association, and as individuals, we often feel divided between the rational and the
emotional, that is, between the limbic system and our neocortex.

According to Jonathan Haidt, social psychology professor at New York University (Stern School of Business) both our rational and our emotional systems are intertwined[5]. He explains this relationship using the concept of the 'rider', the rational mind, and the 'elephant', the emotional mind. While the rational rider appears to be in control, the emotional elephant is powerful and enormous and will win whenever there is a disagreement between them. The elephant represents our limbic system and includes emotions, gut feelings, and visceral responses. The rider our neocortex, by contrast, has very little influence on behaviour. Although the rider can look into the future, imagine hypothetical scenarios, and make plans, he cannot order the elephant to do anything, he can only suggest or advise a particular course of action. Usually, we don't realise this and we think that we are in charge of the elephant. Sometimes we don't even realise there is an elephant, and then we become surprised when we don't stick to our plans and don't do what we know we "should" be doing. The analytical rider's ability to strategize for long-term goals can easily be hindered by the emotional elephant's desire for instant gratification. This has profound implications for managing and developing sales forces.

AUTOMATIC (ELEPHANT)

intuition

fast, easy ....indefatigable

"hot" - connected to motivations, reward centers

99% of all cognition

CONTROLLED (RIDER)

reasoning, language, logic

slow, effortful...tires out

"cool" - not connected to motivational centres

1% of all cognition

Source: Jonathan Haidt, 2007, The Happiness Hypothesis: Putting Ancient Wisdom to the Test of Modern Science

COACHING AND MANAGING SALES PEOPLE

The rider-elephant metaphor is useful to understand why despite sales managers' best intentions to develop their people, some coaching approaches they employ may not work. For instance, sales managers often accompany a sales person to sales meetings with customers. The purpose of these joint visits is to provide feedback with a view of improving the quality and business outcomes of the seller-customer interaction. Coaching and observations of one or a few sales interactions may not work. Developing individual relationships with customers and selling large or complex solutions requires developing nuanced insights about the customer context, awareness of past conversations and understanding the unique personalities of the customer's decision making unit. In such a context, sales managers may better help develop sales person's effectiveness by engaging with their sales people in regular discussions of account relationship development strategies, qualification of new opportunities, projected financial returns aiming etc. This is different and may have more positive and long-lasting effects than evaluating behaviours in discrete sales meetings. To avoid coaching discussions deteriorating into an evaluation of anecdotal buyer-seller episodes, high levels of detailed information, in-depth understanding of the customer business context and the sales person's attitudes are needed for a meaningful review of individual performance in sales. A number of models exist to help sales managers conduct effective coaching interventions. A popular one is the GROW model to help sales managers to structure coaching sessions[6]. While the model brings structure to a coaching conversation, it emphasizes the rational discussion between the sales manager and the sales person. The discussion is often largely focused on the 'rider'. By the end of the session, the sales person understands what is above or below expectation, and eventually what he or she should be doing to rectify the situation. But then nothing, or very little, happens in terms of behavioural or mind-set change. Sales Managers have expressed their frustration when the difference they seek to make through coaching is minimal or inexistent.

CHECKLIST

We often notice that performance reviews are just an extension of the monitoring process whereby the sales manager asks the questions and writes everything down in order to better understand what is happening. During such sessions very little attention is given to the role of the sales manager as a facilitator helping his or her sales people to gain more experience or to increase their motivation.

How much do you as a sales manager facilitate your sales people to gain more understanding of what they are doing and thereby become more experienced?

Have a one-to-one review with one or several of your sales people. After the session complete together with your sale
person the following checklist:

 1. *Who did all the writing during the session, you or the sales person?*

 2. *Who did most of the talking, you or the sales person?*

 3. *What new insights or knowledge does the sales person have now as opposed to before the session?*

 4. *Have you agreed clear actions that the sales person must follow up on?*

 5. *Has the person written the agreed actions down ?*

 6. *How are you going to follow up on it?*

 7. *Has the sales person given you commitment about the actions he or she will perform?*

 8. *Have you at any time summarised what was said and agreed upon during the meeting?*

We have seen sales managers argue that their sales people do not understand the need to plan and execute sales strategies, or that sales people are reluctant to change or even unwilling to modify their behaviours. We have knowledge about a case of a sales manager who devised a mathematical formula in an attempt to convince his sales team to adopt a particular behaviour in sales meetings. The problem is that elephants do not care about reason let alone mathematical formulas. As Jay A. Conger claims in this work on persuasion: "numbers do not make an emotional impact, but stories and vivid language do"[7]. It is like telling a smoker that smoking is not good for him using statistics of the chances of developing cancer and even dying. It is unlikely to work!

Using sophisticated techniques to frame and agree meaningful and on important goals in a coaching session will often induce a feeling of empowerment in the sales person and motivation to exert efforts towards achieving these goals, thus increasing the levels of expectancy. Having regular and coachee-centred sessions may create a bond that acts as a subtle catalyst for the sales person to ensure that the goals agreed are actually accomplished: a powerful way to reduce procrastination. The timing between individual coaching sessions is also an important factor to consider. There must be enough time in between for the sales person to have been able to complete the goals agreed in the last sessions, or at least sufficient time so actions can be initiated. Focusing on the thought processes behind formulating goals will have long-term positive impact and enhance ownership of the follow up actions. Ask your sales executives to provide a summary of what was said and agreed and ask them to elicit both the personal and the organisational barriers they perceive in achieving the agreed goals. This will foster stronger commitment to undertake the required actions. Writing down and publicly committing to our actions is another powerful persuasion technique as Robert Cialdini's decades of research has shown[8]. A public commitment from the sales person should be followed by a sales manager's commitment to help the sales person to undertake the agreed actions. If a sales person decided not to respond positively to this approach, then the consequences of being perceived as untrustworthy, inconsistent and ungrateful for the help received would be so severe that most would 'rider' the 'elephant' to the agreed destination, despite the elephant's tendency to wander about or to procrastinate.

GROW

GOAL	>	REALITY	>	OBSTACLE	>	WAY FORWARD

What are the goals or targets of the sales person?

What has been achieved so far? How far are we from reaching our goals?

What are the obstacles in our way and what are the options available to us to overcome them?

What actions are we going to perform to reach our goals?

EXAMPLE: *THE GROW PROCESS*

Whether you do it in a group or in a one-to-one setting the GROW approach to conduct coaching interventions fits the principles mentioned earlier very well. GROW can be used in a coaching meeting between a sales manager and the sales team, in addressing an individual performance challenge or in working to pursue a specific business opportunity. The GROW model provides a simple (yet not simplistic) effective, and structured methodology for coaching in sales performance and problem solving contexts.

THE PROCESS

GROW stands for Goal, Reality, Obstacles (and options) and Way forward which represent the different stages of the process. The first step is to define or identify what the goals are. The second step consists of how far we are from reaching these goals. This will lead you identifying a set of problems to be addressed. For each problem, you need to ensure that you find the root cause in order to ensure you are not addressing the symptoms. Problems, or in this case obstacles, can often be solved in more than one-way. Based on the list of options to address, you will need to select which one to tackle in order to move forward.

IT IS SIMPLE.

The power of GROW is that it is easily understood, straightforward to apply and systematic. The GROW Model enables you to break down an issue into its constituent parts. Once these are clear, it becomes straightforward to develop solutions.

IT WORKS.

Using GROW the participants create solutions themselves, so it is likely they will be committed to carrying them through. GROW has been tested on thousands of occasions with promising results in short time scales. In addition, once you have an understanding of how it works, it is possible to apply it to a variety of issues in a very effective way.

HOW TO USE THE GROW MODEL?

A one page document containing the different steps of the GROW model is enough to apply the model in practice.

The topics of the discussion are located in the first column and they vary depending on the type of sales activity the sales person performs. Once you have defined the types of topics to discuss you can start filling in the template document together with the person you coach. For each topic, you discuss the goal, the results until now, the obstacles that are in his way and the best way forward to reach the goals.

For instance, an insurance company who uses direct selling to promote their products employs the method to coach both their sales people and sales managers. As their sales people gradually recruit their own team members, they move slowly from selling to managing. Their weekly coaching must therefore adapt from sales activities towards how they coach and how they manage their team. In order to help them structure and standardise their coaching approach they have adopted the GROW model.

In the case of this insurance company, the sales target for the team is divided among the team members. They further divide the targets by month to focus on short-term objectives. At the start of the meeting, the coachee writes down the names of all the team members in the first column followed by their sales targets for that month.

In the column results, the coachee fills in the actual sales results of each sales person for that month together with the expected results based on the outstanding proposals. The sum of the actual and the forecasted results in comparison with the targets indicates whether there is a problem with that sales person or not (or perhaps the forecast!).

For those people who have a problem, the coach and the coachee discuss the obstacle(s) that is preventing this person from reaching the assigned target. They identify the options to overcome this obstacle and select one of them as the way forward in managing this sales person.

The same process also works for other sales organisations. The unit of analysis changes from sales people to sales opportunities or customers.

ARE WE REALLY MOTIVATED BY SELF-INTEREST?

We now return to the fundamental issue of motivation in a quest to decipher behaviours in sales and customer management contexts. In a social and organisational setting, people who do not collaborate, also known as 'free riders', can be very dysfunctional. As a result, to protect ourselves, organisations have developed systems assuming we all tend to behave like free riders when the situation allows doing so. The paradoxes underpinning certain decisions have been studied using game theory. Game theory dictates how to make decisions in a strategic setting and was originally used in economics and political science. One famous approach in game theory is the Nash equilibrium developed by John Nash and portrayed in the Hollywood movie "A Beautiful Mind". It is said that the Nash equilibrium is reached when all players have decided on their strategy and that no other player can benefit from changing their strategy after considering the opponents strategies. This is commonly known as the prisoner's dilemma.

THE PRISONER'S DILEMMA

Two criminals, suspected to have robbed a bank, are arrested and imprisoned. They are kept in separate cells and have no means to communicate with each other. The police do not have enough evidence to convict them on the principal charge. They offer each prisoner an alternative. If they testify against their partner they will go free while the partner will get five years in prison. If they both testify against each other, they will get two years in prison and if they both refuse to testify, each one will receive a 1-year sentence in prison. Both criminals would be better off if they both refuse to testify. However, the theory assumes both criminals will only think about themselves. In this case, the Nash equilibrium is reached when they both decide to testify against each other. This is because even when they know the strategy of the other they cannot improve their own.

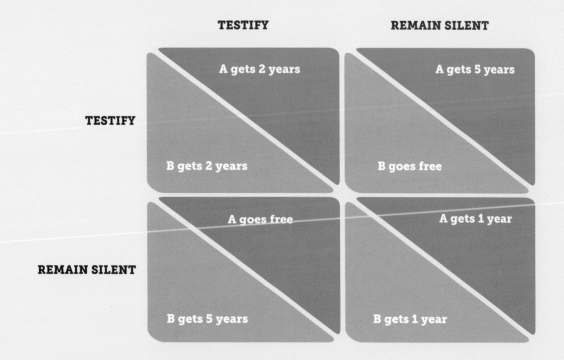

	TESTIFY	REMAIN SILENT
TESTIFY	A gets 2 years / B gets 2 years	A gets 5 years / B goes free
REMAIN SILENT	A goes free / B gets 5 years	A gets 1 year / B gets 1 year

PRISONER A   PRISONER B

THE COMMON GOOD EXPERIMENT

Game theory is useful to analyse decision making in situations where if one party wins the other one loses, also known as zero-sum games. Free riding, or taking advantage of the others, is the dominant strategy in the Nash equilibrium. The aim is to make decisions to ensure that no one can take advantage even though that may not lead to the best decision overall. Another game is called the Public Good Experiment, which is different from the prisoner dilemma game theory because the externalities are positive instead of negative. The more you collaborate, the better the outcome. Let us look at an example:

Four people are brought into a room and seated at a table. Each of the individuals is given an endowment of €5. They are then told that they can choose to keep some money privately for themselves and invest some or all of their €5 in a group project. In particular each participant will simultaneously and without discussion put an amount between €0 and €5 in an envelope. The organiser collects all the envelopes and calculates the total amount the participants'

contribute to the group project. He or she then doubles the total and divides it over the four participants in the group. No one except the experimenter knows the others' contributions, but all know the total.

According to the Nash Equilibrium, the best option would be not to contribute. If others contribute, you win and if others do not contribute you are at least not worse off. The best option would be for all the participants to put in their €5 euro to the group project. If they do that it will generate €20 for the project which when doubled and divided by four ensures each participant €10 in return. However, one participant can choose not to contribute anything to the group project. This means that the total of €15 doubled and divided by four gets everyone €7,5. The one who did not contribute wins the most as he or she ends up with €5 plus €7,5 from the group total which is €12,5. The worst option is that no one contributes anything. The question now is "How would you behave?".

WHY DO PEOPLE COLLABORATE?

50%
Collaborate

30%
Free Riders

20%
Opportunists

Why would people voluntarily contribute to the public good when they are incentivised to free ride is something that has been puzzling economists for some time. The public good experiment helps to shed some light on that question. There is an ever-growing body of research on the subject of voluntary contribution to public good, which contradicts the assumption that we are only driven by self-interest. The research shows that 50% of the participants systematically and predictively collaborate, 30% behave selfishly (free riders) and the remaining 20% are unpredictable[9]. There is also growing evidence that self-interested individuals will choose to collaborate out of a feeling of reciprocity and the need for preserving or building a reputation. These studies do not reject entirely the notion that people are motivated by self-interest. However, they show that self-interest is only one of the elements that explain human motivation.

When building sales management systems we need to ensure that they are consistent with sales people's social or collaborative needs, as well as to their need to improve themselves individually. We need to take into account that the majority of sales people want to collaborate and that those who are driven by self-interest will eventually adapt their behaviour and will collaborate as well. This leads to the question of how can we develop a sales management approach centred on and encouraging collaboration?

THE COLLABORATIVE FRAMEWORK

The reversed logic of sales creates a new form of collaborative selling leading to a more complex and less structured sales process involving team-based selling approaches. Traditional forms of sales management based on well-crafted sales processes and incentives may no longer be appropriate. During our research we noticed that a number of organisations have already abandoned the practice of motivating their sales force with financial rewards exclusively. Only those organisations whose sales force was still involved in simple transactional sales processes used commission-based salaries as a means to motivate their sales people. All the other organisations used a combination of fixed salary with a bonus paid usually at the end of the year. However, the bonus was rarely mentioned as a means to motivate. In almost all the cases, the bonus was part of the overall reward system for all the employees of the organisation, which compensate the overall contribution made by these individuals to the business.

The design of reward systems also needs to adhere to principles of fairness and consistency as well as alignment with reward and performance management systems. The aim is for the reward system to be perceived as a fair system whereby all employees benefit from the organisation's performance and their individual achievement rather than just a control/motivation mechanism. As a result, sales leaders need to incorporate into their practices and processes, tools to appeal to the self-interest of their sales people but also their collaborative intent. They can stimulate collaborative behaviour by fostering a sense of common purpose and by raising the levels of engagement of their sales people.

There is a growing amount of research showing that
the level of collaboration between individuals is driven by:

01. THE AVAILABILITY TO **COMMUNICATE** WITH EACH OTHER,

02. THE WAY IN WHICH TASKS ARE **FRAMED**,

03. THE PRESENCE OF **PUNISHMENTS** AND **REWARDS**,

04. THE EXTENT TO WHICH INFORMATION AND DECISIONS ARE MADE
OPEN AND **TRANSPARENT** AND,

05. THE AMOUNT OF **AUTONOMY** THEY EXPERIENCE PERFORMING
THEIR TASKS.

We will now look into each element of our framework
together with some case examples of sales organisations

COMMUNICATION

An important element in the case of the prisoner's dilemma is that the criminals cannot talk to one another. However, if they could communicate, how would that affect the outcome? Rationally, communication should make no difference to the outcome. Even if both criminals make promises and commitments to each other, they may break these for the sake of self-interest. In real life, this would mean that people constantly break the promises they make to each other. That is not the case. It has been found that opportunities for communication significantly raise the cooperation rate in collective efforts. In many cases, people's focus on their own self-interest is a direct result of a co-ordination failure. If people could get together and co-ordinate their activities they would, more often than not, collaborate[10]. So, as a sales manager or a key account manager how could you facilitate the communication between your own teams and your customers?

One sales manager in a financial institution told us they provide all their sales people with a "LinkedIn" account with access to user groups restricted only to their sales people. The aim is to motivate their sales people to share best practices and to communicate with each other. They also assisted their sales people on how to use social media in their daily work. In many ways, this is a first step towards helping their sales people to create their own personal brand on the Internet. A move which is led by the fact that more and more prospects "Google" for information about the organisation and the sales person who is calling on them prior to accepting a meeting.

Sharing information is often one of the main benefits claimed for the use of a CRM system. However, they are often regarded as a reporting, rather than a knowledge-sharing, system. For that reason one organisation replaced their CRM system with an intranet portal system. It changed the internal perception of the aim of the system focusing on information sharing rather than on reporting. As a direct result, employees started using the system, which soon afterwards was used throughout the whole organisation as a collaboration and information-sharing platform. This is also valid for Key Account Managers who must help their own team members to network as much as possible within the customer's organisation. Many organisations we work with use stakeholder analysis as part of their key account plans. The aim is to map out who should speak to whom, how these individual relationships could be improved, and how to maintain regularity of interactions amongst each other. Very often, communicating with the people involved in the operational work leads to the identification of new opportunities. Once spotted, these opportunities can be discussed with executives who are more senior. The role of the key account manager with established accounts is often not to sell but to ensure that both teams (suppliers and customers) are working well together. In key customer relationships, it is not unusual to have a supplier manager looking after and co-ordinating all the activities with the vendor's key account manager.

FACE TO FACE INTERACTION

When people are able to communicate, they tend to become more empathic and more trusting. Research shows that face-to-face is far superior to any other form of communication. This may be due to cues obtained from facial expression, tone of voice, body language, and removal of anonymity. Research based on MRI scans showed how people's brains responded differently when they interacted with a computer versus with a person, even though the outcome was the same[11]. The more solidarity and empathy we feel for others the more likely we are to take their needs and interests into account.

HOW CAN YOU GET PEOPLE TO FEEL MORE SOLIDARITY FOR EACH OTHER?

A couple of years ago we worked with a large organisation that was organised into business units, each selling and servicing their own products. Each business unit was responsible for their own profit and loss accounts and employed their own sales people. In order

to leverage cross selling, they implemented a CRM system through which sales people could exchange leads with one another. The results were however, rather disappointing. Sales people rarely exchanged any leads. They did not even inquire as to whether customers had any other needs, which could be fulfilled with products from other business units. The organisation introduced new incentives in their performance management system in order to motivate the sales people to exchange leads amongst one another. Yet, this did not deliver any improved results. One manager said, "before we were organised in business units all our sales people worked out of the same offices, spread around the different countries. Back then it was common practice for sales people to exchange leads. Why can't we organise this today through our CRM system?" A plausible explanation to this phenomenon is that in the past, sales people knew each other personally. As a result, they would help each other out and pass on leads to each other on a regular basis. The organisation started to run face to face networking events and organised joint training programmes to ensure that all the sales people and sales managers across the organisation came to know each other personally. As a result, sales people started to network internally which did result in an increase of leads being exchanged.

Question: H[...]
foster more o[...]
communic[...]
the sales fo[...]
con[...]

w could you
ollaboration/
tion within
ces in your
ext?

FRAMING

In 2004, researchers at Stanford University conducted a research project called "Wall Street / Community Game"[12]. The game was a simple prisoner's dilemma game. One group of people were told the game was called the "community game" and another group was told the game was called "the Wall Street game". Out of the total, 70% of the people playing in the group that was told they were playing the 'Community Game' collaborated, whereas 30% who were told they were playing the Wall Street game did actually collaborate. Similar studies based on the Public Good Experiment showed similar results. These studies show how people care about the purpose of their work or the act of doing something good for others. Even though the outcome of the experiment is the same, people respond differently to how it is framed. This concept is also referred to as "Warm Glow". Participants collaborate not just, because they care about each other, but because they care about the purpose of the end results.

According to a Gartner report in 2013 , the IT analytics and consulting firm, only 10% of social collaboration projects succeed due to a lack of purpose[13]. They investigated the social collaboration efforts of more than one thousand organisations and concluded that one of the main problems is the lack of purpose. This is due to a "provide and pray approach" which provides access to a social collaboration technology and prays something good comes of it. The purpose must resonate with the participants and draw them to collaborate and engage with others creating a sense of community. For several years, we have worked with an insurance organisation that uses a multi-level marketing system to acquire new customers. This form of selling is also known as direct selling whereby all the sales people are self-employed and operate in a pyramid-like structure. In order to move upwards in the hierarchy, they need to achieve very specific sales targets within one semester. These targets require them to recruit, train and manage sales people of their own. Since all the sales people are self-employed and paid only on commission, according to the self-interest theory they should all be highly motivated and constantly trying to achieve the highest amount of sales commissions. However, in this company, this was not the case. This example illustrates that in order to move up in the hierarchy sales people need to motivate and pull all their sales people underneath them together and make them work towards a common goal. The sales person going for the promotion needs to work hard during a whole semester motivating their sales people to work as hard as they can.

Why would anyone work harder and give up some of their personal time in order for someone else to achieve their promotion?

From the perspective of self-interest, you would conclude that by working harder they would sell more and therefore earn more commission, even though they do not get the promotion. Therefore, there is win-win. If this were true, why would the sales people not always work as hard as they can? The reality is that when someone decides to go for their next promotion the community underneath them pulls together and collaborates to make it happen. When the person achieves their promotion the whole team celebrates and communicates it with pride and a sense of achievement.

The irony is that direct selling is grounded in the belief that people act only driven by self-interest. Therefore, the organisation constantly aims to motivate their direct sales force through a myriad of incentives and commissions. In other words, they frame it as a 'Wall Street' game. This delivers the base line performance of the organisation. However, outstanding results are achieved only when sales people within the direct sales force decide to go for their next promotion and rally and focus in achieving the common objective: the 'community game'.

Question: How do you **frame your** [...] **order to ins**[...] **community** [...] **sales p**[...]

ow can you
bjectives in
il a sense of
within your
eople?

PUNISHMENTS & REWARDS

People care not only about their own wellbeing but also about the wellbeing of others. This is referred to as altruism. However, research shows that the reality is more complex than that. People care about others in relation to how generous others are[14]. When playing the Public Good Experiment game several times in a row you notice that the degree of collaboration decreases over time. This is the result of people adjusting downwards their levels of collaboration over time to counter the behaviour of the free riders in the group. This is due to the sentiment of unfairness, which is created by the free riders among the group. However, allowing participants to punish those who do not collaborate can change this trend in the game. By adding a rule to the game by which players can punish other players for low contributions or reward others for high contributions, collaboration does increase. So, the same people who care about other altruistic people also hurt other people who hurt them. If someone is nice to you, fairness dictates that you will be nice to them. If someone hurts you, then based on fairness some may feel legitimised to hurt them back.

We judge fairness in a relative way, usually in comparison with our peers. True fairness would be where everyone has the same, or there is an equitable system of balance, such as where those who work harder get more than those who are lazy. In other words, people want to be rewarded fairly or equitably for their performance and they will compare their rewards with those of their colleagues or sales people from other organisations. We often notice when surveying the engagement levels of sales people that high performers are less satisfied with their rewards than their colleagues. This is often explained by the fact that they feel the organisation does not sufficiently recognise their contribution.

In a matrix organisation, we often see that people use their degree of collaboration as a means to punish or reward others. In one organisation, we had access to, technical pre-sales people would deliberately avoid collaborating with sales people who they felt were taking advantage of them. Sales people who were perceived to be unfair, would constantly find it difficult to obtain technical assistance for their customers. This may be seen as an extreme way to 'punish' colleagues considered unfair. Another means is through a 360-degree feedback system as revealed by members of an organisation for which we

HOW DO YOU ENSURE EVERYONE IS WELL AWARE OF THE RULES AND NORMS WHEN COLLABORATING BOTH INTERNALLY AND EXTERNALLY?

administered such evaluation.

Communication by itself may not be enough to enforce certain behaviours in groups and within organizations. There must be consequences for those who break promises and commitments. Therefore, implementing mutually accepted rules for individual conduct, and imposing sanctions on those who violate them can encourage co-operation. One technology research organisation which participated in our research regularly co-create new products and services with its customers. With every new project or customer, they go through a very formal legal process to agree upfront with the customer who will have what type of rights to further commercialise the outcome of their collaboration projects. This way they minimise the dysfunctional effects of free riding or the prisoner's dilemma.

Another manufacturing organisation told us they lost customers because of commercialising a product they initially developed with its customers. The fact that the supplier took the product and turned it into a commercial product created a sense of 'unfair appropriation' in the customer who initially helped to develop such product. They punished the organisation by ending their relationship and started working with one of their competitors. As a result, the manufacturer has now adapted their approach and ensures they have formal agreements in place with their customers to share the benefits of co-creation.

Question: H
sales people
who do not
or do not
behaviour t

ow can your
unish others
collaborate
xhibit the
ney expect?

TRANSPARENCY

Through communication and interaction, people constantly redefine their preferences, principles and goals. Therefore, the more people that interact and communicate, the more they influence each other to collaborate. Experiments have also shown that telling all individuals who has contributed, and how much they have contributed, makes a difference to contributions. People tend to adapt how much they collaborate to how much others collaborate. This is also referred to as reciprocity and comprises the family of strategies that are based on the expectation that people will respond to each other in kind. In group situations reciprocity can be a very effective means to promote and sustain cooperative behaviour. By contributing, subjects build a reputation as co-operators, causing reciprocal subjects to increase their own contributions. Reputation refers to the view of others towards a person. In situations demanding collective action, people might make judgements on a person's reliability and trustworthiness based

on his or her reputation. This is also referred to as consistency. People have a desire to appear consistent in their beliefs, views and behaviour. By making people's views and promises known to everyone, they will feel compelled to adapt their behaviour in order to appear consistent and trustworthy to the others.

One organisation we worked with wanted to make everybody's sales performance targets and their progress more transparent and more 'top of mind'. They started using a shared Excel spreadsheet, which detailed the individual targets and agreements, and how far they were from accomplishing them. The problem was that the shared spreadsheet was perceived more as an administrative burden than as a tool to increase the transparency and the motivation for people to perform. The organisation started looking for a better system and found some tools online called social performance management tools. These tools allow teams of people to set their targets and report their progress on a real time basis. Every time something is updated, the rest of the team is notified. They implemented such a system because they saw it as a way to keep targets and achievements 'top of mind' among their sales people in their daily work. By breaking the overall targets down to smaller, almost daily targets, they are able to keep the dialogue flowing among all their sales people. In their view, by having their sales people publicly communicating their targets and reporting their progress they are committing themselves to the organisation but also to each other. According to Dr. Robert Cialdini's principles of persuasion, we are driven by the need to remain consistent with our previously held views, and our declared intents. This is driven by the need to be seen as trustworthy and reliable. The more publicly you express your views, the more you will be driven to stick to them, thus increasing your perception of transparency and trustworthiness by others.

Question: How increase the transparency sales p

w could you
e degree of
among your
eople?

AUTONOMY

One large European electronics manufacturer implemented a very strict and controlled opportunity qualification process. For each opportunity the manufacturer's enterprise sales people have to complete a whole set of documents which are used by their managers to decide whether to pursue an opportunity or not. This decision has to be taken/revised almost at each step of the processes. As a result, autonomy is taken away from the sales person with regards to which opportunity they want to pursue and how they want to do it. When we met with executives from this company, they were confronted with the problem that their sales people avoided selling solutions and focused primarily on 'safer' and more predicable product selling mode. By focusing their activities towards selling their products, the sales people were able to manage the whole process themselves without requiring the need of a solution engineer. According to the sales managers, the sales people were not used to collaborate with other colleagues during their sales process. The amount of additional paper work and formal approvals to get the support from solution engineers discouraged them to pursue selling solutions that are more complex. This example illustrates that in certain contexts by removing all the autonomy from the sales,

may contribute to more predictable and compliant processes, but also limit people's willingness to engage in more sophisticated consultative selling approaches.

THE SOMA PUZZLE

Research shows that when employees experience a sufficient amount of autonomy in performing their work they develop higher levels of trust with the organisation, have less concern about pay and benefits, and display higher levels of satisfaction and morale[15]. Motivating people by giving them more autonomy is something which is very counter intuitive. Instead, organisations often provide them with incentives. Psychologist Edward Deci conducted research with two groups to see the effect of extrinsic rewards on learning. Group one was paid for solving a puzzle called SOMA; the second group received nothing. Afterwards, both groups were left alone and observed. The group that was paid stopped playing; the group that was not paid kept playing. Deci summarised his findings as: "Stop the pay, stop the play." He further concludes, that monetary rewards undermined people's intrinsic motivation. Rewards seemed to turn the act of playing into something that was controlled from the outside: It turned play into work, and the player into a pawn. Rewards and recognition are important, but as the research has shown, when rewards or awards are used as a means of motivating people, they can backfire.

Traditionally, managing the effectiveness of the sales force focused primarily on processes and their outcomes, as well as on measurable facts. As discussed earlier in this chapter this form of management requires stable and predictable processes. The fast pace of change in many industries and need for more customer centric sales approaches are making this management approach no longer suitable. As a manger, you need to rely much more on the judgment of your sales people, who need to take ownership of their targets, and on the working practices of the people. If we want sales people to adopt a mind-set based on co-creating solutions with their customer it has to start within the organisation itself. In other words we have to co-create sales force effectiveness with the sales people. This means giving them a reasonable degree of autonomy and ownership in defining their objectives and targets and how they wish to achieve them. By involving all the sales managers and sales people in improving and developing the effectiveness of the sales force, it will help create a feeling of ownership of the changes that are chosen. This will enhance the likelihood of seamless implementation. Good ideas that are not supported by those who have to carry it out, stands very little chance of being implemented.

SOMA PUZZLE EXPERIMENT

	DAY 1	DAY 2	DAY 3
GROUP A	No reward	Reward	No reward
GROUP B	No reward	No reward	No reward

HOW DO YOU PROVIDE AUTONOMY TO YOUR SALES PEOPLE?

You provide autonomy to your sales people by allowing them to play a role in the decision-making. For instance, why not let people define their own sales targets? People have tasks or activities that they have to perform. However, why not leave the choice of how they perform their activities to them? When it is time to evaluate your sales people's performance, why not allow them to evaluate themselves and come up with their own conclusions and recommendations? In our experience, managers do not only need to provide choice, they also need to encourage people to participate in the process of decision making. Often sales people need help and structure on how to do that.

The case of target setting involving employees is not new. Participative goal setting is one of the main principles behind management by objectives (MBO). Advocates of MBO claim that when employees are involved in the goal-setting process and in choosing how to achieve the goals, they are more likely to fulfil their responsibilities. They also have a clearer understanding of the roles and responsibilities expected of them. Not everybody agrees with this view. Some claim that many employees do not want to share the responsibility to set targets and that they see that as the senior manager's responsibility. Others claim that these participative goal-setting processes are mere tactics for the top management to 'sell' their targets to the employees. There is also still a considerable amount of debate amongst the research communities as to whether participative versus assigned goals are better and whether they lead to higher performance.

Some studies have shown that assigned goals produce results comparable to, or even better than, participative goals, However, other studies conclude that assigned goals lead to higher levels of employee satisfaction. In our view, the key is in how you organise the participative goal-setting process. It is essential that the whole process not only appeals to the rider (the rational side) but also to the elephant (the emotional side). If not, sales people while committing formally to the goals will procrastinate and delay any action to achieve them. We therefore believe that participative goal setting can help to motivate sales people. By combining both the sales planning and the goal setting process, sales people are obliged to think about how they are going to achieve their goals, thereby raising their levels of expectancy. By having sales people publicly presenting and even defending their sales plans they are committing themselves. We are driven by the need to remain consistent with our previously held views. People wish to be seen as trustworthy and reliable. The more publicly you state your views the more you will be driven to act consistent with them. In our experience, it is also essential to break the activities into smaller units of time, which could be months or quarters in order to offset the element of delay.

In order to increase sales' people motivation and performance, another option is to allow them to define certain aspects of their own job. Why not allow people to define for themselves how they wish to accomplish their objectives? One technology research and development organisation schedules workshops asking their business development managers to work together and to develop individual account plans for their customer. The aim is to have people collaborating on different account plans to challenge each other. This also allows them to discover different approaches from each other and even some cross-selling opportunities. The aim of the exercise is to develop a set of objectives for each account and a strategy for how to achieve it.
The result is an overview document of the overall account development strategy, which can be presented and discussed with other colleagues, managers and even the customer. The sales managers take the initiative to organise the workshop, what happens during the workshop and the end result is left to the business developers who decide among themselves how to best approach and develop their customers.

Question: Ho
area could yo
amount of a
sales peop

w or in which
u increase the
tonomy your
e receive?

SUMMARY

SALES MANAGEMENT APPROACHES HAVE TRADITIONALLY BEEN CATEGORISED AS MAINLY ACTIVITY FOCUSED OR RESULT FOCUSED.

ACTIVITY BASED APPROACH

An activity based approach favours the view that our pursuit of self-interest will eventually lead to our own downfall, therefore our behaviour needs to be controlled. Such an approach is also based on the belief that the organisation knows best which sales activities the sales people should perform in order to achieve the expected results. This type of strategy relies on a high amount of close monitoring and coaching of sales people. It also requires an atmosphere in which the sales people accept high levels of control on their activities. The advantage of this approach is that it allows sales people to engage in activities which are not always revenue-generating activities but necessary to drive the business. This type of approach is typically associated with managing existing customers where, besides selling, the sales people have to engage in a number of other service-related activities. The disadvantage of this approach is that it lacks focus on outcomes and requires well-defined sales processes which can be monitored and measured accurately. This approach is therefore best suited for highly repetitive sales processes operating in a predictable environment, requiring little or no creativity on the part of the sales person.

RESULT BASED APPROACH

This view favours a result based management approach, which is based on the belief that the only true measure of a salesperson's performance is the results he or she produces. The market will determine the sales people who will be successful and those who will not. How the sales person achieves their results is completely irrelevant, only the results count, and that is what they will be rewarded on. Because the activities the sales people decide to engage in are entirely their own responsibility, they also require very little guidance and monitoring. Measuring sales results is both factual and objective, thus making objective setting and performance evaluations straightforward processes with low level of bias and personal interpretation. This type of strategy is believed to make the sales person fully accountable for her/his performance. To do this it provides the sales person with full control over how they will achieve their performance. The disadvantages of this approach is that it leads to short-term thinking and results can be correctly attributed to the right sales person, making it very difficult to use in team selling environments.

SELECTING THE RIGHT APPROACH FOR YOU

Most sales managers use a hybrid form combining elements of both approaches when managing their sales force. Nevertheless, one approach usually dominates and this is based on the organisation's ability to measure outcomes as well as the activities that are to be performed.

Is the organisation able to measure **sales activities** accurately and completely?		Is the organisation able to measure **sales results** accurately and completely?	
		YES	**NO**
	YES	RESULT BASED OR ACTIVITY BASED	ACTIVITY BASED
	NO	RESULT BASED	?

THE THIRD OPTION

With co-creation, sales people do not have predicable sales processes and the organization relies on their ability to be creative in terms of how they engage with customers and partners. As co-creation implies, the process involves many internal and external stakeholders, which means that any sales results are likely to be a joint effort of several people, making it difficult, not to say impossible to attribute them to one individual. We therefore need a third sales management approach. The third alternative management system is one that favours collaborative team and group-based systems.

COLLABORATIVE BASED APPROACH

Collaborative-based sales management approach is based on the belief that if everyone is equally concerned with the well being of the organisation, they will all behave and perform to the best of their abilities. This mechanism is based on an informal social system that ensures people will naturally operate towards the objective. The more sales people are trying to move in the right direction, the less supervision you need. In the attempt to deal with complex social and political conflicts, the control system develops techniques such as teamwork and employee participation in decision-making. These models emphasise the notion of quality of working in the accomplishment of the set goals and objectives.

The values and beliefs of the organisational culture play a vital role in the operation of these control systems. It has been established that the greater the interdependence between departments to get a task completed, the greater the use of a collaboration-based management approach, which confirms the importance of this approach for team based selling and co-creation.

IMPLICATIONS: THE HYBRID APPROACH

In this book, we are not advocating that we should stop using outcome or even activity targets. On average, 30% of us are free riders and 20% behave opportunistically and this needs to be controlled. What we are advocating is that we need to create a hybrid sales management approach not only based on activities and outcomes but also based on collaboration. Current advances in information technology combined with the fact that most organisations today rely heavily on information technology to function, makes an organisation that is not able to measure any form of outcome or behaviour very rare. For that reason we advocate that the primary form of sales management should be based on collaboration and the secondary based on (traditional) measures.

		Is the organisation able to measure **sales results** accurately and completely?	
		YES	NO
Is the organisation able to measure **sales activities** accurately and completely?	YES	*RESULT BASED OR ACTIVITY BASED OR COLLABORATION BASED*	*ACTIVITY BASED OR COLLABORATION BASED*
	NO	*RESULT BASED OR COLLABORATION BASED*	*COLLABORATION BASED*

WHAT COLLABORATIVE MANAGEMENT IS NOT

A phrase we often hear is "it is more complicated to get something sold internally than to sell it to a customer". In fact, in some industries we noticed that key account managers only stay in their role for a relatively short length of time. They suffer from burnouts or get frustrated by the amount of stress associated with these roles and leave. Of course, this is not the case everywhere. In one cross- industry survey we performed in 2012 we noticed that those account managers who are satisfied with their job indicate they have a much better understanding of their role, experience fewer role conflicts and receive adequate coaching from their management. In our experience management attention, call it supervision or coaching, is the most important factor.

This new form of collaborative management with emphasis on collaboration, intrinsic motivation together with autonomy does not mean that hard targets are not important anymore, nor that people no longer need to be managed. Within many organisations we visited and worked with, we noticed that targets were still used but people were more often than not left on their own, receiving little management attention at all. No matter how high or low you are in the organisational hierarchy we all procrastinate. This is also why sales managers who claim their sales people are all high end professionals and therefore do not need to be coached or managed are wrong. (This is usually the rational explanation of the sales manager who chooses to perform other tasks than coaching or managing his people. We all procrastinate!) One important role of the sales manager is to help their sales people to stick to their plans and not slip into spending their time and effort on the wrong activities. While we advocate more collaborative forms of management over the old command and control approach, we also warn that there is a risk of going too far. Some form of command and control is needed in order to stay on the path and avoid procrastination. The difference is that yesterday sales people were told what to do; today they are reminded to stick to what they agreed to. Within complex matrix organisations people do experience problems understanding what their roles and responsibilities are in relation to their colleagues. This often leads to conflicts and sales people need sales managers to help them but also to coach them whilst becoming more experienced in their jobs.

MECHANISMS	MOTIVATION	WORLDVIEW	SOURCE
Autonomy	Pure Altruism	"I am motivated to ensure we all improve ourselves"	Intrinsic Motivation
Framing	Altruism (Warm Glow)	"I am motivated by the purpose of our work"	Intrinsic Motivation
Punishments	Fairness	"I will punish those who try to free ride"	Intrinsic Motivation
Transparency and Communication	Desire for Approval	"I want others to see and appreciate what I am doing"	Intrinsic Motivation
Transparency and Communication	Reciprocity	"If I do not reciprocate I feel guilty."	Intrinsic Motivation
Punishments and Reward	Formal Incentives	"I want to avoid being punished and risk losing everything"	Extrinsic Motivation

Chapter 6
FROM A JOB TO A CALLING

WHAT IS THE IMPORTANCE OF INTRINSIC MOTIVATION?

Selling today is a team effort and will be even more so in the future as customers operations grow in complexity. The underlying assumption for the collaborative management approach to work is that ideally most sales people will be primarily motivated by intrinsic motives. Your goal as a manager is to leverage this motivation and to allow individuals to flourish and achieve high performance in a collaborative work environment. However, the reality is that, far from all your sales people are intrinsically motivated. This raises the question about the reasons why they are not intrinsically motivated and what can be done about it? A large degree of energy towards motivating people should go into demonstrating to them how their actions will lead to results.

Effective motivational approaches tend to be both process-focused as well as people-focused. Think about this scenario, imagine that a business is seeing its sales figures going down. This organisation turn to sales training programmes to improve their sales people's skills. By improving their skills, it is believed that their activities will be better performed thereby improving the expected results. The assumption is that people are motivated by their work and that they want to find ways to become even better at what they do. Through standardised sales processes and training, many organisations seek to help their sales people to accomplish the company's goals.

LOW INTRINSIC MOTIVATION LEVELS
HIGH INTRINSIC MOTIVATION LEVELS

ORGANISATIONAL
COMMITMENT

SALES
PERFORMANCE

1   2   3   4   5

Source: Satisfaction Survey of Sales People, 2012, Sales Cubes

This approach however, may still be limited. Decreasing sales often reveal new competitive market conditions that need to be considered, but also internal practices that may need to be revisited. These are sales managers' responsibilities that require addressing resistance to change in sales forces as well as in the management team. Revitalised sales strategies require more holistic key performance measures and incentives. However, the long-term effectiveness of sales performance enhancement calls for tackling people's intrinsic motivation at work. Long-lasting interventions in sales organisations need to be mindful of the environment in which sales people work, and define specific roles and responsibilities accordingly. For instance, the complexity of managing existing customer relations in some industries means that it is unfeasible to ask sales people to also focus on acquiring new customers. Conversely, in some types of sales, maintaining the customers that one has acquired is appropriate and advisable. Good sales force designs take in consideration both the internal and external context when defining the role of the sales person. A meaningful role definition will enhance intrinsic motivation. Over the years, our sales force effectiveness surveys, have demonstrated a clear link between sales people's levels of intrinsic motivation and their performance and organisational commitment.

Why do sales people display such different levels of intrinsic motivation in their work? Many sales people will refer to the work they perform as their career, some will see their work in sales as just a job; others may have found their calling and believe that through their work they make a contribution that they feel is meaningful and significant. One of the reasons why sales people see their work so differently stems from how they became a sales person in the first place. In the past, the sales profession was one possible option for people without formal education to have a chance to initiate a career in business. Today, selling and account management is not yet widely taught at business schools and remains seen in the eyes of many as a vocation rather than a profession. So, why do people often choose a career in sales despite having a university education? We often hear about people in sales who come from other functions (e.g. operations, technical or customer service). In some companies, it is an unwritten rule that to be considered for a high managerial position, individuals have to have some commercial experience.

These days, we increasingly hear sales managers telling that after recruiting a sales professional, they need to demonstrate that new sales people are productive very quickly. The pressure to deliver and the difficulty to find adequate candidates sometimes lead organisations to appoint people in sales positions from other departments. For these people a job in sales is an opportunity to do something else and a way to improve their salaries. With the emphasis, shifting from the ability to persuade others to the ability to provide expert advice, the move towards a career in sales is becoming an option for people who were holding positions in other functions within their organisations. In order to achieve high levels of performance, individuals require a mix of knowledge and expertise about the company's offerings and a customer-centric attitude.

Over the last few decades, we have seen a decrease in operational / transactional sales roles that are increasingly performed by call centres and/or Internet web sites. The remaining sales forces are gradually considered as middle and top level, evidenced by a growing number of strategic sales roles such as business development managers, key account managers, or tactical roles such as solution and product architects. These roles give sales people with more autonomy to co-develop solutions with customers and partners while also providing them with more authority to command resources within the organisation. The blurring of boundaries between suppliers and customer and the invitation to customers to collaborate means that organisations no longer have full control over all the activities and their sequence in the sales process. This implies that the sales organisation relies much more on the creativity and abilities of the individual sales person than on a standardised sales process. To improve the effectiveness of a sales force, organisations need to focus more on developing the right work attitudes, by defining job requirements that are in accord with the internal and the external context of the business and the motivations of individuals.

WHAT ARE DIFFERENCES BETWEEN JOB, CAREER AND CALLING?

For most people, work constitutes a large part of their life. Therefore, job satisfaction greatly influences their quality of life. According to Amy Wrzesniewski , Professor of Psychology at Yale Business School, how people view their work, plays an important part in their overall satisfaction and also in their personal happiness[1]. She believes that people perceive their work either as a job, a career or a calling.

People who have a job are primarily interested by the money they earn and do not normally seek any other types of rewards from it. They see a job as a means to support their life outside their work. If they were financially secure they would not continue with their job, though they may not be necessarily unhappy in their work. In some instances, we have even seen some of these people refuse extra responsibilities because they do not expect anything more out of their job.

People who have a career are much more engaged in their work and seek more than just financial rewards such a promotion, power and prestige. While they may enjoy their current work they do not expect to be in the same position in the next couple of years. As soon as opportunities for promotion stop, they loose their satisfaction and tend to leave. It is either moving up or moving out. Staying inevitably affects their self-esteem, which would lead them to see their work as a job. They are willing to accept work, which may seem a waste of time, knowing that this position will allow them to move further on. They believe that the next promotion will bring them happiness. Paradoxically, as soon as they have reached the next position, a new and higher position is already waiting for them. This never-ending quest to reach goals in order to find happiness leads to a 'rat race' whereby happiness is an illusion that they may never reach.

People who have a calling see their work as a passion and it is an integral part of their life. They do not just work for money or promotion but instead for the sense of satisfaction and fulfilment that doing the work brings to them. It's a vital part of who they are. They take their work home and on vacation too. To others, they may appear as workaholics but for them work in itself is a source of energy and motivation. They see their work contributing to the greater good, to something bigger than themselves. They would be upset if they were forced to stop working and retire. Often when forced to retire they establish themselves as self-employed professionals.

"The most beautiful fate, the most wonderful good fortune that can happen to any human being, is to be paid for doing that which he passionately loves to do."

Abraham Maslow

	JOB	CAREER	CALLING
DRIVE	*Money*	*Power and Status*	*Contribution*
WORK OUTLOOK	*Work is a necessary evil*	*Can't wait to get to the top*	*Vacation / Mastery*
EAGER TO	*Have a vacation and to retirement*	*Next position*	*Contribute to the better world*

Job-Career-Calling is not dependent upon one's occupation. We can, therefore, find sales people who, in the same job, have completely different types of perceptions of their work. How people perceive their work has a great impact on how they will perform.

For professional sales people, Job-Career-Calling is not dependent upon the type of sales roles. We are led to believe that sales people in more managerial functions such as key account management will be more intrinsically motivated in their work than a sales representative who performs a more operational role. In one industry-wide survey, performed by Sales Cubes, management consulting organisation, in 2012 we noticed some large differences between people's

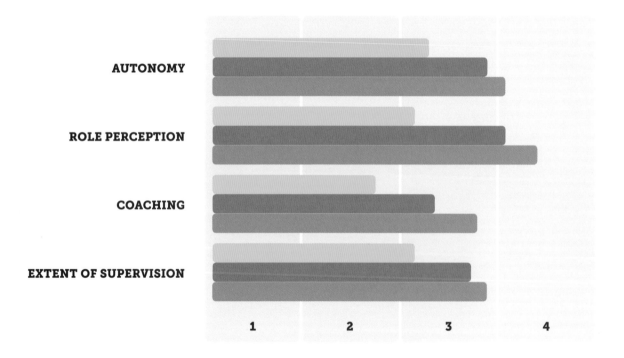

JOB CAREER **CALLING**   Source: Satisfaction Survey of Sales People, 2012, Sales Cubes

attitudes towards their work and their roles within the sales organisation. Surprisingly, sales people in simpler sales roles, for instance demonstrating capability to call on many customers a week, reported much higher levels of motivation than their colleagues in managerial sales roles such as key account or sales managers. Not only are these sales people more motivated they also report much higher levels of job satisfaction and organisational commitment.

Job-Career-Calling is not a typology like personality traits. It is very tempting to categorise people along these three mind-sets. Unlike personality, the mind-set can be changed. Changes in an organisation can create or remove opportunities altering sales people's perceptions of their own work. The relationship between the sales person and his manager plays a very important part in deciding the way the sales person perceives his job. In our consulting practice, we often conduct surveys within and across sales organisations. In one such cross-industry survey the data revealed distinct differences in their work attitudes, and a relationship between these and the amount of direction and coaching sales people received.

The extent to which managers coach and provide supervision to their sales people greatly influences the sales people's perception of their own roles and amount of autonomy. If a sales person does not clearly understand what is expected of them, or does not know how much autonomy he has to fulfil her/his role, the individual will rarely be able to fully develop competencies for that role. In many sales organisations roles change constantly as people leave and new people come. Tasks and responsibilities are continuously being shuffled within the sales force. Because it is not step change but more a constant evolution of the job, sales people are not always conscious or aware about how they perceive their own job. Coaching and frequent interactions with their managers help sales people to deal with the required understanding of their roles and to reshape them when needed in a quest of maximising contribution and performance.

The process of analysing a role and reshaping it is a technique called job crafting. In our view this technique can help sales people and their managers to find a better fit between the individual and the job, leading to higher levels of intrinsic motivation.

Read each paragraph carefully before scoring. Once you have read the three paragraphs rate yourself for each of them:

MR. A works primary to earn enough money to support his life outside of his job. If he was financially secure, he would no longer continue with his current line of work, but would really rather do something else instead. Mr. A's job is a necessity of life, a lot like breathing or sleeping. He often wishes the time would pass more quickly at work. He greatly anticipates weekends and vacations. If Mr. A lived, his life over again, he probably would not go into the same line of work. He would not encourage his friends and children to enter his line of work. Mr. A is very eager to retire.

MR. B basically enjoys his work, but does not expect to be in his current job five years from now. Instead, he plans to move on to a better, higher level job. He has several goals for his future pertaining to the positions he would eventually like to hold. Sometimes his work seems a waste of time, but he knows that he must do sufficiently well in his current position in order to move on. Mr. B can't wait to get a promotion. For him, a promotion means recognition of his good work, and is a sign of his success in competition with his co-workers.

MR. C 's work is one of the most important parts of his life. He is very pleased that he is in this line of work. Because what he does for a living is a vital part of who he is, it is one of the first things he tells people about himself. He tends to take his work home with him and on vacations, too. The majority of his friends are from his place of employment, and he belongs to several organizations and clubs relating to his work. Mr. C feels good about his work because he loves it, and because he thinks, it makes the world a better place. He would encourage his friends and children to enter his line of work. Mr. C would be upset if he was forced to stop working, and he is not particularly looking forward to retirement.

Not at all like him/her	A little like him/her	Somewhat like him/her	Very much like him/her
1	**2**	**3**	**4**

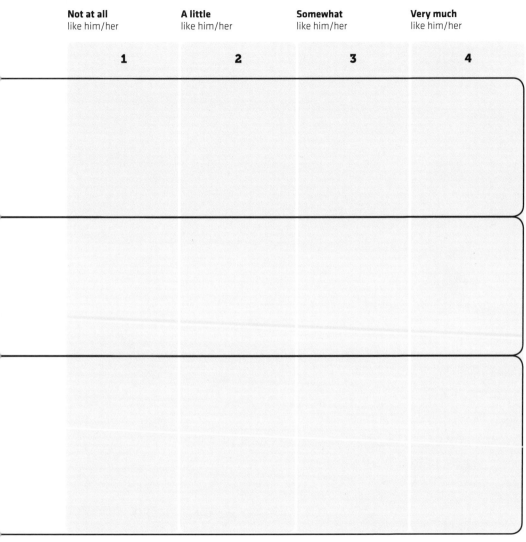

Source: Amy Wrzesniewski, Clark McCauley, Paul Rozin, Barry Schwartz, "Jobs, Careers, and Callings: People's Relations to Their Work" JOURNAL OF RESEARCH IN PERSONALITY, 1997[2]

SCORING

Answers to the questionnaire.
Which of the three characters **Mr. A**,
Mr B or **Mr C** received the highest score?

MR A: *JOB*
MR. B: *CAREER*
MR. C: *CALLING*

EXAMPLE
JOB CRAFTING

Sales Job Crafting is a process by which the participants analyse the content of their day-to-day work with the aim to find a better fit between their strengths, motives and passion and the nature of the work assigned to them. The scope of the exercise is to help sales people make changes while staying within the boundaries of their work. It is based on the notion that sales people have a certain degree of autonomy to define how they perform their work enabling them to craft their job. The analysis may help sales people to find opportunities to make their job more engaging and fulfilling. So, job crafting is not about redesigning the job but rather about reorganising the work itself, and in a way that is more satisfying for the sales person. Changes can be brought to the job in the form of changes to the tasks they perform, the colleagues they work with, the customers they serve, or even the context within which they perform their work. Simply changing some of the tasks, relationships or the context of the work also changes the meaning of the work itself.

In terms of motivation, job crafting may help to increase the value sales people place on their work by linking it with their personal motives and passions. Linking their work more closely with their personal strengths also raises their expectancy that their effort will produce the desired results. An increasing number of organisations are using participative goal setting as a way to get their sales people more involved in the process and make the goals more acceptable. Similarly, job crafting invites sales people to participate in the design of their job. There are many different techniques that can be applied to allow sales people to craft certain aspects of their work.

Amy Wrzesniewski at the Yale School of Management has been studying "job crafting" for more than a decade and proposed the 'Job Crafting Exercise', an example of which is provided below. Inspired by her work, we have further developed exercises and methods and used them in sales with very positive results.

Maria is a young ambitious sales person working for an insurance organisation. Executives within the organisation have identified Maria as a potential future sales manager. They have started coaching her towards her future new role. They promoted her to team manager allowing her to recruit new junior sales people and to coach them into their role. As a team manager, she has to juggle her time between her role as a sales person and as a team leader. Recent events are showing she is struggling with her new duties of recruiting and coaching junior sales people. Two of the people she recruited left shortly after they joined the company. Although being disappointed by recent events she was able to maintain satisfactory sales results. In an attempt to help her to manage her priorities and tasks, she was chosen to participate in one of our job crafting exercises. As a result of the session she realised that she was actually pursuing the wrong goals. Using Maria's case we will demonstrate how sales people can craft their own sales jobs.

ANALYSING CURRENT TASKS AND ACTIVITIES

In preparation for the session, Maria was asked to review all the tasks scheduled in her agenda for the last couple of months and to list her 10 main tasks.

ACTIVITIES 1 TO 10

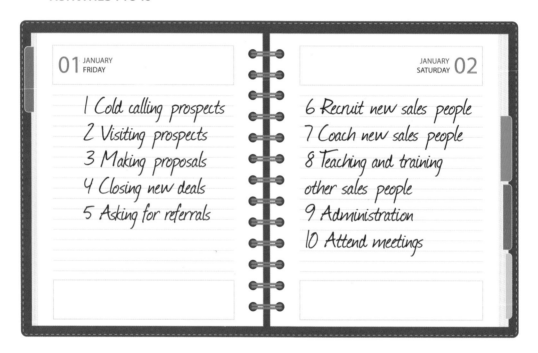

01 JANUARY
FRIDAY

1 Cold calling prospects
2 Visiting prospects
3 Making proposals
4 Closing new deals
5 Asking for referrals

JANUARY
SATURDAY **02**

6 Recruit new sales people
7 Coach new sales people
8 Teaching and training other sales people
9 Administration
10 Attend meetings

Using this list she organised them into three groups, large, medium and small, based on the time she spent on them.

LARGE AMOUNT
OF YOUR TIME

Visiting prospects

Closing new deals

MEDIUM AMOUNT
OF YOUR TIME

Cold calling prospects

Making proposals

Attend meetings

SMALL AMOUNT
OF YOUR TIME

Asking for referrals

Recruit new sales people

Coach new sales people

Teaching and training other sales people

Administration

IDENTIFY THE PURPOSE OF YOUR WORK

Based on the tasks in front of her she then started analysing who were the main people affected by her job and its outcomes. The objective of this exercise is to be conscious about the actual contribution of one's job and how other people are affected by it. It helps to redefine the value of some of our tasks allowing us to see them in a better light.

Who		How
Sales Manager	→	Become the manager
Me and my partner		Income
Customer		Service I render
Junior Sales People		Coaching

When Maria presented the purpose of her work, she stated that becoming a sales manager was something that she was doing to please her manager. This triggered a discussion with one of the directors who participated in the session. He argued that if she did not want to become a sales manager she should not do it. Maria looked confused and ended the discussion by saying she did not express herself correctly.

WEAKNESSES, DISLIKES AND BORES

As part of the analysis, Maria started analysing her strengths, passions and motives. Because identifying one's own strength is difficult for some people. We invited the participants in the groups to say what they admired the most in each of the other participants. Beside the fact that it creates a good atmosphere, which will foster discussions that are more open, it also helps to identify what you are good at.
Based on the comments Maria received from her colleagues she developed the following list:

Having analysed the good sides Maria also identified elements of her job she really disliked and elements she felt she was not good at.

MOTIVES

Develop a career	Meeting new people	Money

STRENGTH

Build rapport with people	Teaching and explaining things to others	Persuading others

PASSIONS

Selling and visiting customers	Teaching

221

DISLIKES

People who do not follow through on their promises	Spending training people who then quit	Internal politics

WEAKNESSES

Telling others what to do	Supervising and monitoring	Recruiting new sales people

MATCHING TASKS WITH STRENGTHS AND WEAKNESSES

Maria reviewed her tasks and asked herself whether the task helped her to achieve her motives, fulfil her passion or whether it utilised one of her strengths. For each match she placed a "+" sign on the task. She also matched her dislikes and weaknesses on each of the tasks by placing a "-"sign.

Maria presented her analysis showing us which tasks allowed her to exercise her stronger points and which were difficult or unsatisfying because they were linked to her weaker points. During the presentation and discussion that followed, she became increasingly self-aware that the role of sales manager she was preparing herself for was not something she really wanted for herself. When confronted with this by the other participants she burst into tears.

She realised that instead of wanting to become a sales manager she should pursue a career as an independent broker, managing a portfolio of customers. However, she regarded the brokers as a lesser function doing a boring job. She admitted that perhaps she knew too little about what it meant to be an independent broker and that she needed to inform herself better.

Visiting
prospects
+ + +

Closing new
deals
+ +

Cold calling
prospects

Making
proposals
+

Attend
meetings
-

223

Asking for
referrals

Recruit new
sales people
-

Coach new
sales people
-

Teaching and
training other
sales people

Administration

After reviewing the following four methods of job crafting
Maria composed a graph of what her ideal job should look
like.

1. Tasks Crafting. Can you change the content of the
tasks itself? Can you increase some aspects or reduce
others? Can you swap the tasks with someone else?

2. Relationship Crafting.. Can you change some of the
people you work with? Can you swap some of your
customers with other sales people? Can you add some
people to your team?

3. Perceptual Crafting. Can you change the way you look
at some parts of your work? Can you learn to accept some
of the parts of your work?

4. Contextual Crafting. Can you change the context
within which you perform some of your tasks?

Analysing Customers Portfolio's

Handling customer requests

Visiting and advising customers

MEDIUM AMOUNT
OF YOUR TIME

Scheduling customer visits

Making proposals

Visiting Prospects

Learning about new products

SMALL AMOUNT
OF YOUR TIME

Asking for referrals

Administration

ROLES AND RESPONSIBILITIES

Having defined which tasks she should be focusing on, Maria went on defining the roles and the responsibilities that came with it. She did this by matching her motives, strengths and passions with the new tasks..

ROLE: SELLING

Scheduling customer visits

Meeting new people

Money

Visiting and advising customers

Asking for referrals

Making proposals

Persuading others

Build rapport with people

Visiting Prospects

ROLE: SERVICING EXISTING CUSTOMER

Analysing Customers Portfolio's

Handling customer requests

Teaching and explaining things to others

ROLE LEARNING ABOUT NEW PRODUCTS

Administration

Learning about new products

Develop a career

Maria planned:

- to contact the sales director responsible for managing the broker network in order to learn more about the brokers.
- to contact one of the most successful independent brokers of the company to visit them and learn about their work.
- to schedule a meeting with her sales manager to inform him about the job crafting session and its outcomes.

Chapter 7
FROM 'AS-IS' TO 'TO-BE'

HOW TO ASSESS A SALES FORCE?

Depending on the industry, organisations we interviewed were at different stages in terms of dealing with the trends presented in chapter one. Typically, manufacturing organisations were only recently experiencing the need to move towards a more consultative selling approach. IT and business consulting organisations, on the other hand, have been already implementing for some years many of the new forms of strategic selling we described. Many organisations recognised a degree of dissatisfaction with the status quo of their current sales practices and strategies. This raises the question, how should businesses upgrade their sales organisations? Which steps should they take first? In this chapter, we will present a method and tools to help you create a vision of your future sales organisation. The aim is to develop a vision of what your sales force should look like in the future and to develop a plan to implement the required transformations

When creating the vision of your sales organisation of the future, we are in essence, looking for ways to increase the effectiveness of the sales force. We define sales force effectiveness as the ability of the sales force to reach its goals in terms of both business results and the development of capabilities. Sales force performance on the other hand is primarily a measure of outcome without necessarily analysing the ways in which that outcome is reached. Sales force effectiveness comprises the performance of the sales force but also the analysis of the ways in which that particular level of performance was reached. So, the purpose of sales force effectiveness is measuring the organisation's sales performance as well as the effort and the results of each individual sales person. Sales force effectiveness can be expressed as the degree to which particular sales objectives are achieved. It can be measured based on outcome and process measures or based on the experiences of the individuals involved.

THE FRAMEWORK

MANAGEMENT

ORGANISATION

SALES PEOPLE

ACTIVITIES

RESULTS

REWARDS

ENGAGEMENT

DESIGN

When we started the research project that underpins the book, we wanted to understand the key issues sales managers were dealing with concerning the achievement of sales force effectiveness. We used validated models of sales force effectiveness to inform the definition of questions to be used in the data gathering of our study. For instance, based on Vroom's expectancy theory, Churchill, Ford and Walker developed and validated a sales-force-effectiveness framework in the late seventies[1]. Since then, the framework has been further developed and validated. Essentially, this framework implies that the higher the salesperson's motivation, the greater the effort, leading to higher performance. This enhanced performance will lead to greater rewards, which will bring about higher job satisfaction. This enhanced satisfaction leads to even higher motivation, thus acting as a loop. The model also implies that if the performance is lower than expected, it will negatively affect the rewards and the person's satisfaction. Since low satisfaction is related to low motivation, it will lead to low effort resulting in a negative spiral. Other elements, outside the control of the sales force, such as the organisation's strategy, products or marketing strategies may affect the motivation of sales people. Sales leaders must, therefore, carefully manage this loop by supervising, training and motivating their sales people. The way in which the sales force is designed, also strongly affects the motivation and levels of effort of the sales force. The business potential of assigned territories and portfolios of customers, and the workload associated to the roles and responsibilities of the sales people, all affect their ability to achieve certain levels of performance.

THE SALES FORCE MAP

The sales force map is a tool we use to easily visualise all the components of a sales force. It provides us with a high level view of how the sales force is organised and which type of market it serves. In one-to-one meetings with a sales manager or in a workshop you can use the map to question specific parts of the organisation and see what could be changed. Because it is based on a cause and effect model, you can also use the map to describe particular problems in a sales organisation and trace back what is causing them.

234

MARKET — ORGANISATION

PERFORMANCE AND REWARDING — MANAGEMENT

CUSTOMER BEHAVIOUR — ORGANISATION

KNOWLEDGE AND COMPETENCIES — SALES PEOPLE

SALES PROCESS — ACTIVITIES

VALUE PROPOSITION — ORGANISATION

ORGANISATION AND DESIGN — DESIGN

The map can be used to describe a current or future situation or even to describe an evolution, for instance describing the changes that happened in the last 5 to 10 years. Each box is completed using a set of questions to trigger the discussion. Typically a list of questions include:

MARKET
What are the trends in your market?

BUYING BEHAVIOUR
What are the trends in your customer buying behaviour?

VALUE PROPOSITION
What are your value propositions and how have they changed over time?

SALES MANAGEMENT
How have these market changes affected the way in which you measure the performance of your sales force?
How have these market changes affected the way in which you motivate and reward your sales force?

SALES PEOPLE
How have these market changes affected the knowledge and skills your sales people need?

SALES PROCESS
How have these market changes affected your sales process?
How have these market changes affected the levels of team work your sales people need engage in to get their job done?

SALES FORCE DESIGN
How have these market changes affected the roles and responsibilities of your sales people?

EXAMPLE FROM AN INTERNATIONAL IT SYSTEM INTEGRATOR

MARKET

ORGANISATION

ICT Market is maturing

Globalisation of customers

CUSTOMER BEHAVIOUR

ORGANISATION

Low Loyalty

Customers are more knowledgeable

Customer consolidates supply base

Increase in shopping behaviour

Centralised purchasing

Looking for business benefits

VALUE PROPOSITION

ORGANISATION

Focus is on business benefits

Sector specific Value Propositions.

More Managed Services type offerings

HOW DOES THAT AFFECT YOUR SALES FORCE?

KNOWLEDGE AND COMPETENCIES

MANAGEMENT

Sector & customer knowledge

More focus on Business Knowledge

More in depth Technology Knowledge

Team Based Selling Skills

Business Consulting type of skills are needed

SALES PROCESS

SALES PEOPLE

More contact persons at one customer

Demonstrate how we have done it before

Setup innovation workshops with customers

Joint Account Planning Activities with the customers

PERFORMANCE AND REWARDING

ACTIVITIES

More use of new media to communicate. with customers

More one to one sessions

Ask customer input to evaluate the performance of a sales person

ORGANISATION AND DESIGN

DESIGN

GAM

Customer / Sector Specialists

Project Management

EXERCISE: HOW TO CREATE A VISION FOR THE FUTURE?

HOW TO MOVE FROM WHERE YOUR SALES FORCE IS NOW TO WHERE IT HAS TO BE IN THE FUTURE?

To develop a roadmap to move a sales organisation from where it is today to where it wishes to be tomorrow, we developed a methodology consisting of four major steps. The first step consists of a current 'As-Is' situational analysis of the sales organisation. The second step consists of describing the future 'To-Be' vision of the sales organisation. The third step consists of a gap analysis between the current 'As-Is' and the future 'To-Be' situation and to identify what needs to be changed. Having identified what needs to be changed a roadmap can be made specifying what needs to be done to make the envisaged change happen, which constitutes the last step of the process. Using a case from the food processing industry (meat), we will demonstrate how an organisation can develop its vision for its sales force of tomorrow. A large producer of high-quality pork and beef products acquired several smaller slaughterhouses in Europe over the last years. The challenge was to incorporate them into a single sales force and to rethink what their added value would be for their customers in the future. In order to help them develop the vision for their sales force of tomorrow, they decided to organise a series of workshops that we briefly describe next.

STEP 1: 'AS IS' ANALYSIS

WHAT IS IT?
An 'as-is' analysis is the analysis of the current situation. The aim is to create a starting point, which all participants can agree on, which will serve as a basis to build the vision for the sales force of the future. All the participants are organised into small groups and are asked to think about how their market and sales organisation have changed over the last five to ten years. It provides a way to identify the main events in the marketplace and how they have affected the sales organization up until now. These events together create the main trends that are affecting the sales force. The analysis also provides insight into why the sales organization looks like it is today.

WHAT CHANGES HAVE HAPPENED IN THE MARKET OVER THE LAST COUPLE OF YEARS?

The case company's market changed significantly over the last decade. The meat industry suffered from several diseases such as foot and mouth and avian flu leading to many governments introducing new policies to improve the safety and quality of the meat. At a social level, health and environmental concerns and growing awareness of animal welfare are influencing the way in which meat is purchased. Market demands and globalization are requiring higher production capacity within the meat processing industry, making it very difficult for smaller slaughterhouses to compete.

HOW HAVE THESE CHANGES AFFECTED THE BUYING BEHAVIOUR OF YOUR CUSTOMERS?

These changes are affecting the buying behaviour of retailers and consumers. In Europe, health-conscious consumers shifting their preferences towards vegetarian diets are affecting the demand for meat. This is largely offset by rising demand in Asia-Pacific. Customers are increasingly looking for transparency in the value chain; they want to know where the meat comes from. There is also growing concern about the welfare of the animal, they want to know how the animal was treated before and during the slaughter process. In contrast, meat is also seen as a commodity product and price is, in most countries, the most important purchasing criteria.

HOW HAS YOUR VALUE PROPOSITION CHANGED OVER THE LAST COUPLE OF YEARS?

They extended their value proposition by providing a quality label that indicates how the farmer treats the animals. This label addresses both the expectation of higher standards of animal welfare by the consumer, but also transparency through the value chain for the retailers and meat processing organisations.

HOW DID ALL THESE CHANGES AFFECT YOUR SALES ORGANISATION?

From a sales force perspective, the changes that affected the company mentioned above meant that in addition to their meat trading activities, they also needed to develop relationships with all the actors in the value chain. This suggested evolving from transactional selling (e.g. meat trading), towards solution / consultative selling (developing relationships and meeting new customer demands in terms of transparency, safety and animal welfare). Because the bulk of the business is still based on trading, sales people had to learn to combine both activities, 'trading' one day and 'consultative selling' the next day, often with the same customer. From a knowledge perspective, the implication is that sales people require more knowledge, first technical about production processes and second about product qualities.

From a sales management perspective, this means that sales leaders' focus is also shifting from monitoring sales trading activities towards helping their sales people to learn new consultative selling skills and to develop solutions with customers. In the past, selling was an integrated part of the operational activities highly linked to the production process. Today, the sales function has evolved to include also business development and relationship management activities. As a result, there is more awareness about the need for a sales culture, with a dedicated structure and roles. Key account managers have been allocated to manage large international customers and to develop tailored solutions for them.

AS IS ANALYSIS

MARKET

ORGANISATION

Increase in health and safety regulations

Growing awareness on environmental impact

Growing awareness on animal welfare

Globalisation and consolidation

CUSTOMER BEHAVIOUR

ORGANISATION

In Europe demand is slowing down

Consumers are conscious more health

Growing demand in Asia

Customers are more concerned with food safety

Customer want more transparency in the chain

VALUE PROPOSITION

ORGANISATION

Quality labels

HOW DOES THAT AFFECT YOUR SALES FORCE?

KNOWLEDGE AND COMPETENCIES

MANAGEMENT

Training the sales force on consultative & solution selling

More focus on solution selling because it is new

SALES PROCESS

SALES PEOPLE

More technical and process knowledge

Product Knowledge

PERFORMANCE AND REWARDING

ACTIVITIES

Finding solutions for customers

Trading

ORGANISATION AND DESIGN

DESIGN

Combined roles of trading and solution development

STEP 2:
'TO BE' ANALYSIS
ANALYSIS

WHAT IS IT?

A 'TO BE' analysis is a way to create a vision of what the future situation will look like. The analysis is based on the same questions as for the 'AS IS' analysis but this time not by looking into the past but by looking into the future. The aim is to identify how the current trends and even possibly new trends are likely to affect your market and your customers. During the exercise, all the participants are asked to think about what the market and the sales organization will look like in the next three to five years. How far you wish to look into the future depends on the type of industry and the type of organisation. We often try to limit the time horizon to a maximum of three years because further than that we find that participants have real difficulties imagining the future participants have real difficulties imagining the future.

HOW DO YOU EXPECT THE TRENDS TO CONTINUE TO AFFECT YOUR MARKET IN THE COMING YEARS?

The global demand for meat products will continue to rise due to a growing middle class population. Globalisation will continue to drive further industrialisation of production processes, which will lead to further consolidation resulting in fewer but larger players in the industry. This will also lead to increasing competition from companies in other continents such as Asia and South America. Intermediaries, wholesalers and small retailers will find it extremely hard to continue to compete and many will be squeezed out of the market. As a result, we may expect to see more vertical integrations between the retailer and the farmer, in order to improve efficiency, but also to provide more transparency and quality control through the value chain. Relationships between the partners in the value chain will become increasingly important. Nevertheless, meat will remain a commodity product, which means that trading, and short-term transactions will continue to dominate the market.

HOW DO YOU EXPECT THESE TRENDS TO AFFECT THE BUYING BEHAVIOUR OF YOUR CUSTOMERS?

We may expect to see more polarisation in terms of buying behaviour between price conscious and quality conscious consumers. Animal welfare and environmental aspects (Go-Green) are expected to be the main drivers to determine the quality of meat. Fashions are also affecting meat products whereby retailers are looking to change more frequently their offerings, shortening the life cycle of meat products.

HOW DO YOU EXPECT THESE TRENDS TO AFFECT YOUR VALUE PROPOSITION IN THE FUTURE?

Meat being a commodity will mean further efficiency gains will have to come from vertical integrations with customers and suppliers.

Part of the value proposition will, therefore, focus on integrating the supplier's production processes with those of the customer in order to gain further efficiencies. On the other hand, the value proposition will also shift towards developing smaller batches of tailor made products allowing retailers to regularly update their products.

For the sales force this means that the scope of the selling activities will grow to include trading, consultative selling and key account management. The growing importance of consultative selling and key account management will also lead to the creation of individual sales roles. From a sales-force design perspective, the sales organisation will evolve towards a more matrix organization whereby account managers will have overall responsibility to manage the customer relationship. Consultative sellers will support the account management to develop tailor-made solutions and the traders will continue to manage the day-to-day trading with the customer.

The activities of the account managers will consist primarily of relationship building and business development. The business development activities will feature a mixture of activities such as: analysing the customer's market, finding ways to co-create new solutions for their customers, and finding new ways to improve the current operations by further integrating production processes. To perform these activities they will need a combination of relationship building skills, business acumen and good knowledge of the production processes in the value chain. The activities of the consultative seller will consist of understanding the customer's needs and translating them into tailor made solutions. The solutions may involve special production or packaging requirements. To perform their activities they will require excellent product and process knowledge as well as good consultative selling skills.

The activities of the traders will consist of selling and negotiating prices with customers mostly remotely (over the phone). They have to combine both products and market demand knowledge. Their challenge consists of ensuring that all the available meat is being sold at the best possible price. Close collaboration between these roles is very important in order to keep the business with the customer profitable. Account managers can, for instance, agree to launch a special promotion for a specific type of meat with their customers. The consultative seller needs to advise how to produce and package and distribute the products. The trader needs to advise on how to sell the other parts of the animal and at what price. The account managers will have a 'management status' meaning they will be mainly managed based on overall team targets and objectives. One key element in their evaluation is their ability to collaborate with colleagues, partners and customers and to develop new business. The solution sellers will be managed based on their ability to find creative and innovative solutions for their customers. The traders will be managed based on their effort and their sales results.

TO BE ANALYSIS

MARKET

ORGANISATION

Demand will grow

More competition from ASIA and Latin America

Intermediaries will be squeezed out

More vertical integration

Further Consolidation

CUSTOMER BEHAVIOUR

ORGANISATION

Some consumers will demand higher quality

Consumer will mainly shop on price

Product will have shorter life cycle. Demand for flexibility in the chain

B2B customers will want more efficiency in the chain

Customer want more transparency in the chain

VALUE PROPOSITION

ORGANISATION

Transparency

Process Integration

Tailor Made Batch Productions

HOW DOES THAT AFFECT YOUR SALES FORCE?

KNOWLEDGE AND COMPETENCIES

Focus on collaboration among the sales forces

Different targets and rewards systems for each individual role

MANAGEMENT

SALES PROCESS

Account Managers: customers, market and prices and supply chain knowledge

Solution Sellers: Product and Technical Knowledge

Traders: Product Knowledge

SALES PEOPLE

PERFORMANCE AND REWARDING

Managing Key Accounts

Solution Selling

Team Based Selling

Spot Trading

ACTIVITIES

ORGANISATION AND DESIGN

Three distinct sales roles

Matrix Sales Organisation

DESIGN

WHAT IS IT?

The aim is to identify what needs to be changed within the sales organization in order to deal with the foreseeable changes in the market for the coming years. During the analysis, the participants are asked to think about all the elements in the sales force that should change. To get the analysis going we use the Four Action Framework, a tool developed by Chan Kim and Renée Mauborgne and published in their book "Blue Ocean Strategy"[2]. Because completing the tool is a challenging task, it drives you to scrutinise every element of your sales organisation, making you discover the range of implicit assumptions you make when designing your sales organisation.

246

BASED ON THE VISION OF THE SALES FORCE IN THE FUTURE WHAT DO WE NEED TO ELIMINATED, REDUCE, INCREASE AND CREATE?

The analysis shows that the company needs to recognise sales as a business function and no longer as an operational part of the production and distribution process. This implies creating a separate sales department. Historically, people evolved into a role in sales after having rotated between several other roles within the production process. As a result, most sales people do not have a business or a sales background. In the future all new sales people will have to be recruited especially for a job in sales. The current practice of having one sales person combining both a role as trader and as account manager will have to be avoided were possible. The profiles and the activities are too different to be performed well by the same person. This means that they will have to restructure their sales organization taking into account two new functions: consultative sellers and account managers together and trader.

Existing sales people will have to be reallocated or new people will have to be recruited to fill these roles. To recruit new sales people detailed role descriptions will have to be made. Subsequently the required process and working practices will have to be created in the organization. As a result, tools and management systems will have to adapted or created to support these new working practices. This will have to be combined with some training programs. When managing the sales force more attention will have to be given to the number of tailored solutions they are proposing to their customers, and the ability to integrate deeper into the value chain of the customers.

ELIMINATE

−

Sales being
part of the
production
function

CREATE

Key Account
Management
Function

New
Recruitment
profiles for sales
people

Solution Seller
Function

Dedicated Sales
Training Program

Tools and
Processes to
support the
new roles

New Sales
Structure

REDUCE

Combined Sales
roles

Promote
production
people into sales
positions

INCREASE

Focus on vertical
integrations with
customers

Recruiting people
with business
background

STEP 4:
GAP ANALYSIS

WHAT IS IT?

The last step consists of generating possible solutions to bridge each of the gaps that were identified. We do this by consolidating the current 'AS IS', 'TO BE' and Gap analysis and complete it with the proposed actions.

TO BE	AS IS	GAP	REMEDY
Key Account Managers coordinating the entire customer related activities and developing new business opportunities with their customers.	The function is currently performed by the existing sales people as an additional responsibility.	Create the function, recruit and train people.	1. Segment customers to identify which one will require a key account manager. 2. Define a comprehensive description of the activities involved in such a role. 3. Pilot test whether such activities do actually add value and whether customers welcome them. 4. Recruit and train accordingly.
Consultative sellers develop and create tailor made solutions.	The function is currently performed by the existing sales people as an additional responsibility.	Create the function, recruit and train people.	1. Define a comprehensive description of the activities involved in such a role. 2. Pilot test whether such activities do actually add value and whether customers welcome them. 3. Recruit or reallocate existing resources

TO BE	AS IS	GAP	REMEDY
Trader focus only on the trading business.	Traders do combine trading, consultative selling and account management.	The function is often combined with other additional roles.	1. Reallocate roles and responsibilities 2. Pilot test whether this change adds value to the sales people and to the customers.
Sales Performance / Management system needs to take into account key account managers and consultative sellers.	Current system is made for traders only.	There is no performance and management system in place defining how to manage key account managers and solution sellers.	1. Define the type of performance targets for each sales role. 2. Define how to set these type of performance target and how to monitor and evaluate them.
Matrix sales organisation focused around key account managers (in the rows) and solutions sellers and traders (in the columns).	Functional organisation.	There is no account management group and solution sellers group. There is no dedicated manager for either group. There are no roles and responsibilities defined for each of the two new functions.	1. Define the roles and responsibilities for each of the sales functions. 2. Define how many sales people are needed in each of the roles. 3. Define who will be managing these people. 4. Allocate people to these roles and communicate it across the organisation and customers.
Develop a sales training program.	There is real dedicated sales training program.	Sales Training program focusing on all three functions.	1. Identity the knowledge and skills needed by each role. 2. Identity existing training programs in the market, which addresses these knowledge and skills areas. 3. Schedule courses.
Formal Account Management and Solution Seller working procedures and tools.	Working procedures and tools do not exist.	Working procedures and tools needed to perform their job.	1. Define clear working procedures for each role. 2. Define which tools and systems the sales people wiii need to use to complete their working procedures.

Chapter 1
FROM PAST TO FUTURE TRENDS

1. Dr. Javier Marcos and Prof. Lynette Ryals, 2011 , Rolls-Royce Civil Aerospace: Meeting Customer Needs with Complex Product Service Offerings, Cranfield School of Management.

Chapter 2
FROM THE OLD TO THE NEW COMMERCIAL LOGIC

1. Neil Rackham, John Devincentis,, 1999, Rethinking the Sales Force, McGraw-Hill.

2. Louis Gerstner, 2003, Who Says Elephants Can't Dance?, HarperBusiness.

3. Jay R. Galbraith,2011, Designing the Customer-Centric Organization, John Wiley & Sons.

4. Henry Chesbrough, 2003, Open innovation: The new imperative for creating and profiting from technology, Harvard Business Press.

5. Steve Blank, 2013, Why the Lean Start-Up Changes Everything, Harvard Business Review, 91(5), 63-72.

Chapter 3
FROM SELLING TO CO-CREATING

1. Robert F. Lusch and Stephen L. Vargo, 2006, The Service Dominant Logic of Marketing, M.E. Sharpe, 3-29.

2. Christian Grönroos and Annika Ravald, 2011, Service as business logic: implications for value creation and marketing, Journal of Service Management, 22(1), 5-22.

3. Lance Bettencourt and Antony Ulwick, 2008, The customer-centered innovation map, Harvard Business Review, 86(5), 109.

4, Chloé Renault, Frédéric Dalsace and Wolfgang Ulaga, 2010, Michelin Fleet Solutions: from Selling Tires to Selling Kilometers, HEC Paris case no. 510-103-1, 2010.

Chapter 4
FROM CUSTOMER TO ASSET MANAGEMENT

1. Gupta, Sunil; Lehman, Donald R, 2007, Managing Customers as Investments, Pearson Education, Inc / Published as Wharton School Publishing.

2. Werner Reinartz and V. Kumar, 2003, The impact of customer relationship characteristics on profitable lifetime duration. Journal of marketing, 77–99.

3. Werner Reinartz and V. Kumar, 2002, The Mismanagement of Customer Loyalty, Harvard Business Review.

4. Sheth JagdishN and Arun Sharma, 1997, Relationship Marketing: An Agenda for Inquiry, Industrial Marketing Management, 26, 2

5. Arun Sharma, 2006, Strategies for maximizing customer equity of low lifetime value customers, Journal of Relationship Marketing, 5(1)

6. C. K. Prahalad, Venkat Ramaswamy, 2004, The Future of Competition: Co-Creating Unique Value With Customers, Harvard Business Review Press.

7. Shapiro, Benson P., Sprint Sell to Close Sales Quickly, Harvard Business School Publishing Case, 2001.

8. Anderson, J.; Kupp, M.,2008, MLP, ESMT European School of Management and Technology

9. Mohanbir Sawhney, 2004, Going Beyond the Product: Defining, Designing and Delivering Customer Solutions Published in Robert F. Lusch, Stephen L, 2006, The Service-Dominant Logic of Marketing: Dialogue, Debate, And Directions, M.E. Sharpe, 365-380.

10. Diana Woodburn, Malcolm McDonald, 2011, Key Account Management: The Definitive Guide, Wiley.

11. Malcolm McDonald, Anthony Millman and Beth Rogers, 1996, Key Account Management - learning from supplier and customer perspectives. Cranfield School of Management: Research report for the Cranfield KAM Best Practice Research Club.

Chapter 5
FROM MANAGING TO COLLABORATING

1. Yochai Benkler, 2011, The Penguin and the Leviathan: The Triumph of Cooperation Over Self-Interest, Crown Business

2. Victor Vroom, 1964, Work and motivation. New York: Wiley.

3. Steven P. Brown, Kenneth R. Evans, Murali K. Mantrala and Goutam Challagalla, 2005, Adapting motivation , control , and compensation research to a new environment, Journal of Personal Selling & Sales Management, 25(2), 155–167.

4. Pierce Steel, 2012, The Procrastination Equation: How to Stop Putting Things Off and Start Getting Stuff Done, Harper Perennial.

5. Jonathan Haidt, 2007, The Happiness Hypothesis: Putting Ancient Wisdom to the Test of Modern Science .

6. John Whitmore , 2009, Coaching for Performance: GROWing Human Potential and Purpose - the Principles and Practice of Coaching and Leadership, Nicholas Brealey Publishing

7. Jay A. Conger, 1998, The necessary art of persuasion, Harvard Business Review, 84–95.

8. Cialdini Robert, 2007, Influence: The Psychology of Persuasion, HarperBusiness

9. Urs Fischbachera, Simon Gachterb, Ernst Fehra,2000 , Are people conditionally cooperative? Evidence from a public goods experiment, Elsevier

10. Olivier Bochet and Louis Putterman,2009 , Not Just Babble: Opening the Black Box of Communication in a Voluntary Contribution Experiment, European Economic Review, Netherlands, Apr 2009 Vol 53 No 3

11. Rilling, J.K., Gutman, D.A., Zeh, T.R., Pagnoni, G., Berns, G.S. & Kilts, C.D. (2002) A neural basis for social cooperation. Neuron 35, 395-405.

12. James Andreoni, 1995, Warm-Glow versus Cold-Prickle: The Effects of Positive and Negative Framing on Cooperation in Experiments,
The Quarterly Journal of Economics, MIT Press, vol. 110(1), pages 1-21, February.

13. Gartner, 2013, Gartner Says the Vast Majority of Social Collaboration Initiatives Fail Due to Lack of Purpose, Press Release Egham, UK, April 2, 2013

14. Sean D'Evelyn, 2010, Private vs. Public Strategies in a Voluntary Contributions Mechanism, http://www.uhero.hawaii.edu/assets/DEvelyn_JMP.pdf

15. Deci Edward,1997, Why We Do What We Do, Penguin Books

Chapter 6
FROM JOB TO CALLING

1. Amy Wrzesniewski, Justin M. Berg and Jane E. Dutton,2010, Turn the Job You Have into the Job You Want, Harvard Business Review • june 2010

2. Amy Wrzesniewski,Clark McCauley, Paul Rozin, Barry Schwartz, "Jobs, Careers, and Callings: People's Relations to Their Work"
Journal of research in personality, 1997

3. Mark Van Vuuren and Luc Dorenbosch, 2011, Mooi Werk, Boom

Chapter 7
FROM AS-IS TO TO-BE

1. Walker, Orville C.; Gilbert A Churchill; Neil M Ford. (1977), "Motivation and Performance in Industrial Selling: Present Knowledge and Needed Research," Journal of Marketing Research, 14(May), 2, 156-168.

2. Chan Kim and Renée Mauborgne, 2005, "Blue Ocean Strategy", Harvard Business Press

RÉGIS LEMMENS,
Phd: **Author**
Régis Lemmens is a consultant,
author and teacher on the topic
of sales and sales management.
He is a partner at Sales Cubes,
a sales management consulting
firm located in Belgium, that
specialises in sales and key
accounts management. He is
a fellow at Cranfield University
in the UK and a he lectures on
sales and sales management at
the TiasNimbas Business School
in the Netherlands.

BILL DONALDSON,
Phd: **Author**
Bill Donaldson is Research Professor
of Marketing at Aberdeen Business
School, Robert Gordon University,
UK. His research interest are in the
management of sales operations
including sales automation and
customer relationship management.

JAVIER MARCOS CUEVAS,
Phd: **Author**
Javier Marcos is a senior lecturer in
Sales Management at the Centre
for Strategic Marketing and Sales at
Cranfield School of Management and
an independent consultant. His main
areas of expertise are Selling and
Sales Management, Organisational
Learning and Organisational
Development. He emphasises the
blend of leading edge research with
innovative training methodologies in
the delivery of his programmes and
the design of consulting and sales
coaching assignments.

MARCO SIMONI,
Graphic Designer
Marco Simoni is a freelance graphic
designer and founder of - S I III O II I
based in Antwerp, Belgium. Marco has
over 6 years experience of making things
look nice.